MW00943351

OTHER BOOKS BY DR. BILL THOMAS

The Eden Alternative

Life Worth Living

Open Hearts Open Minds

In the Arms of Elders

What are Old People For?

Tribes of Eden

Second Wind

Principia Senescentis

MESH

Move-Eat-Sleep-Heal

Dr. Bill Thomas

SANA Publishing

Published by Sana Publications
714 N. Aurora St., Ithaca, NY 14850

Cover Art by Jude and Bill Thomas
Designed by Kyrié Carpenter
Illustrated by Sami Pelton
Icons by IconGeek26, SmashIcons and FreePik from www.flaticon.com

Thomas, William H.
MESH: Move-Eat-Sleep-Heal

Non-Fiction
Aging
Philosophy
The text for this book is set in Verdana
Manufactured in the United States

This book is dedicated to
Haleigh and Hannah Thomas.
They taught us how to heal.

MOVE
EAT
SLEEP
HEAL

Contents

Introduction

Sometimes something very wrong can show us the way toward something very right. The "health care system" we know today is very wrong.

Lifespark founder Joel Theisen, RN, calls it a "sick care system," and it is hard to argue with him on this point. While awareness of the negative consequences of hospitalization and intensive medical treatment continues to grow, attempts to improve the acute care system's ability to care for old people have made little progress. Not coincidentally, the policies and programs that finance health care services remain tilted heavily in favor of impersonal, high tech, and in-patient services. They invest very little in keeping old people healthy and at home. What if we took a hard look at what's going wrong and used those insights to show us how to make things right?

Many research studies have shown that when old people are hospitalized, they are likely to be discharged in a weakened state, sleep-deprived, undernourished, and exhausted. Doctors refer to this phenomenon as **"post-hospital" syndrome.**

This state of fatigue and frailty is an unintended consequence of the acute care system's ferocious focus on diseases and its disregard for people. Young people are better able to tolerate this kind of mistreatment because they arrive at the hospital door with youthful reserves of stamina. Old people, in contrast, often undergo life-changing losses of strength, balance, and endurance -- even when their medical condition has been treated effectively.

This book examines "post-hospital" syndrome in a new light. Instead of mourning the health care system's inability to care for the whole person, it asks: "What simple things make the biggest positive difference in the health and well-being of old people?"

Common sense, bolstered by rigorous research, tells us that people -- including people who are old -- need to MESH:

Move
Eat
Sleep and
Heal

In a 2013 editorial published in the New England Journal of Medicine, Dr. Harlan Krumholz observed that, in addition to enduring an acute illness or injury, hospitalized patients are also:

"...commonly deprived of

sleep, experience disruption of normal circadian rhythms, are nourished poorly, have pain and discomfort, confront a baffling array of mentally challenging situations, receive medications that can alter cognition and physical function, and become deconditioned by bed rest or inactivity."

As one of America's leading geriatricians, Krumholz recognized how dangerous and debilitating these situations are and called for the health care system to:

"...more assertively apply interventions aimed at reducing disruptions in sleep, minimizing pain and stress, promoting good nutrition and addressing nutritional deficiencies, optimizing the use of sedatives, promoting

practices that reduce the risk of delirium and confusion, emphasizing physical activity and strength maintenance or improvement, and enhancing cognitive and physical function."[1]

This is sound advice, to be sure, but in the years since his article was published, little has changed. All of the studies Krumholz cites are well known. The interventions he advocates are well established. The need to address re-hospitalization is currently thought to be urgent. Even so, the problems he describes grow worse by the year. Why?

Krumholz's unquestioned acceptance of the historical practice of hospitalizing older people when they are ill or injured makes it hard for him to arrive at his paper's most natural and satisfying conclusion. The most effective way to eliminate "Post-Hospital Syndrome" is to stop unnecessarily admitting older people to the hospital.

The modern hospital is specifically and energetically engineered to focus on the admitting diagnosis. Hospitals can respond effectively to many severe acute illnesses and injuries. However, they are ill-equipped for the task of helping people living with chronic conditions. What's missing is an abiding concern for the well-being of the person living with the diagnosis. If hospitals insist on making people weak, hungry, tired, and anxious, it is up to us to explore new (and old) ways of fostering strength, purpose, and belonging.

Hospitals are proverbial leopards, powerful and dangerous. They have shown little interest in changing their "spots." We, however, are free to adapt our own beliefs and practices.

We can choose to do the simplest and most important things -- better. Happily, the MESH (Move, Eat, Sleep, Heal) approach to health and wellness makes use of modern medicine's most effective tools and insights while keeping the person at the center of our attention. MESH focuses on our urgent need to move, eat, sleep and heal, rather than obsessing about pills and procedures.

Advocates of in-patient medicine will declare that this inverts the natural order of things. They will insist that the "presenting complaint" must take precedence over the person.

This book "flips the sick-care script." Instead of trying to reform acute care, it asks how we can avoid hospital-system care? After all, no one wants to be a patient.

No one wants:

- Medical treatment
- Diagnostic tests
- Hospitalization or
- Surgical procedures

We want to be healthy and happy. We do our best to avoid medical and surgical interventions whenever it seems safe to do so.

We want:

- Well-being
- Health
- Love and
- The ability to do good work

MESH (Move, Eat, Sleep, Heal) focuses on us and what we want. MESH connects moving, eating, sleeping, and healing to health and well-being in a new way. MESH offers us a chance to build strength, purpose, and belonging for ourselves and help others do the same. It can help us reduce our contact with the "sick care system" and spend more time living the life we have chosen for ourselves.

There is nothing magic about MESH. It is grounded in science and distilled common sense. It will not make us younger or wipe away our wrinkles. MESH can offer a gift of great value. It helps us be better at being old. For thousands of years, people have searched, fruitlessly, for a "fountain of youth" that heals all ills. All that time, the fountain of age stood right in front of us. We can drink from it any time we choose. Its name is MESH.

Aging versus Anti-Aging

In most airports, there is a room set aside for pilots to use when developing their flight plans. In some rooms is a placard that reads: "Remember: The Law of Gravity Will Be Strictly Enforced." Our ability to soar above the clouds, higher than any eagle would dare to fly, is a wonder of the modern world. But gravity never rests. Something like this is true about aging. More people than ever before are living longer and better than our ancestors could have dreamed possible. Living longer means aging more because aging, like gravity, never rests.

Every now and then, we are gifted with a "flying dream" that lets us soar into the sky using our arms like wings. Science fiction movies often feature gadgets with blinking lights that, somehow, let heroes turn gravity on and off at will.

Inventors with wild hair and wilder ambitions tell us that a practical anti-gravity machine is just around the corner. But we know that dreams are dreams, movies are movies, and that the inventors' high hopes are bound to be dashed. It's the same with anti-aging. The dream of being young forever is delicious as can be.

The reality is that each and every day of our lives, we wake up one day older.
This is the iron Law of Aging.
The Law of Aging, like the Law of Gravity, is strictly enforced.

The Fountain of Youth

Just about everyone wishes they could shed a few pounds, have a little more energy or have a little less gray.

Aging can be irksome. Accordingly, some people place their faith in and do their best to pursue a life based on the principles of anti-aging. For them, youth is the only path to health and happiness.

Anti-aging advocate Aubrey DeGrey is one of those people. He predicts a scientific breakthrough that will allow people in their 70s and 80s to be "rejuvenated" to the age of 30 or 40. Even better, you will remain unchanged by time. "So your risk of death each year is not related to how long ago you were born, it's the same as a young adult. Today, that's less than 1 in 1000 per year, and that number is going to go down as we get self-driving cars and all that, so actually [a lifespan of] 1,000 [years] is a very conservative number."[2]

The wish for a long, youthful life is common enough. What makes anti-aging advocates different is their vision of aging as a bitterly unjust, unnatural, and immoral imposition on humanity. They see perfection in youth and want to extend that perfection indefinitely.

The problem is that humans do get old, and aging is as certain a thing as death and taxes.

Of all the humans who have ever lived, not one has ever grown young.

Anti-aging advocates continue to promise us a technological breakthrough that will defeat aging forever and, who knows, maybe someday their dreams will come true. Until then, we will keep waking up one day older.

Most spokespeople for the anti-aging philosophy temper their enthusiasm a little more carefully. Michael F. Roizen, M.D.'s "age reduction program" was supposed to make the people who use it "live and feel up to 26 years younger." He counsels, "We must stop thinking about health as the prevention of disease and start thinking about it as the prevention of aging." His book, *RealAge: Are you as young as you could be?*, offers readers sensible advice on how to reduce one's risk of developing many of the diseases commonly associated with old age. He recommends stopping smoking, losing weight, being physically active, lowering stress levels, and eating a healthy diet. Everyone should do these things, if they can.

What is interesting about Roizen's work is not the content of his recommendations, which are in the mainstream of preventive medicine, but the reason he gives for why they should be adopted. "The better condition you are in—that is, the younger you stay—the better prepared you will be to fight the factors that age you. When you take care of your body, time slows down."

Roizen's book was first published in 1999, and we can now say, with certainty, that time has not slowed down. In 2008 Roizen claimed that, within five years, a medical breakthrough would likely allow people to "live until 160 with the same quality of life as at age 45."[3] The fact is that not one of his readers stopped being old or started being young. Each morning they wake up one day older than they were the day before.

Aging is a reality. Anti-aging is a dream.

People have dreamed of magic water with the power to reverse aging for thousands of years. The Roman historian Herodotus shared this fascination. He wrote of a people (living in present-day Somalia) who, he believed, lived 120 years or more. According to Herodotus, these people ate only flesh and drank only milk. Their longevity was said to be due to a fountain that made the skin of those who washed in its waters glossy and sleek. Daily use of this water kept the people young. Or so it was said.[4]

Two thousand years later, King Vakhtang Gorgasal was hunting in the forests of what is now the nation of Georgia. His falcon caught a pheasant but dropped its prey which fell into a hot spring. When it touched the water, the bird became well again and flew away. Astonished, the king immediately gave orders to build a city on this site. The city's modern name is Tbilisi, and while the city is still famed for its hot springs, they no longer appear to heal mortal wounds.[5]

A thousand years later, Ponce de Leon became the first European to set foot on what would become the continental United States. He called the land Florida. While there were local legends of a fountain that "made old men into boys," it is unlikely that de Leon believed the stories.

His primary interest was money and the mines and plantations (worked by people he had enslaved) that made him wealthy. DeLeon wanted to be richer still. But, when he returned to Florida and attempted to establish a permanent settlement, the Calusa (they called themselves the "fierce people") resisted and wounded him in battle. He died soon after, at the age of 47.

Five hundred years later, the "Fountain of Youth Archaeological Park" operates as a privately owned tourist attraction in St. Augustine, Florida. Each year, tens of thousands of visitors come to sample the fountain's water. According to one former park employee, it does not taste good. "Imagine what you would think the Fountain of Youth would taste like. It doesn't taste like that." A tourist describes the fountain's waters as smelling like sulfur and tasting "like it had been used to wash pirates' dirty socks."[6] Somewhat ironically, the Fountain of Youth Park offers discounted tickets to seniors.

Living in a modern age we are no longer fascinated by fountains with magic anti-aging water. Now we look to science and pseudo-science for the miracles that can keep us young forever. We seek "hope in a bottle" and the free market is happy to oblige us. Sleek, glossy skin, which we associate with youth can be had, for a price. By 2014, our fear of wrinkles had morphed into an anti-aging industry worth $261.9 billion.[7] Some of the products on offer make King Gorgasal's faith in bird restoring hot springs seem quite sensible.

Writing on the website Bustle.com, Kristen Collins Jackson notes that, "For women in particular, however, a youthful glow and smooth skin can seem essential for applying for certain jobs, dating, and just getting people to smile at you in the street. Which is exactly why some of these insanely peculiar anti-aging treatments exist."[8]

- **Urine Therapy Claim:** "Using your own morning urine for a facial provides essential nutrients that heal discoloration and skin pigmentation issues that come as we age."

- **Bee Venom Skincare Claim:** "Its anti-inflammatory properties are said to temporarily firm the skin producing a more youthful look."
- **Sheep Placenta Facial Claim:** "The youthful glow it brings out lasts for 30 days because of the nutrients in sheep's placenta."
- **Snail Secretions Claim:** "Compounds in snail slime significantly reduce wrinkles."
- **Fire Facials Claim:** "An alcohol soaked cloth set ablaze for 'just a few seconds' is said to decrease skin sagging and wrinkles."

The point here is not to mock those who would resort to "urine therapy" to conceal signs of aging but rather to ask why they would choose to do so. Aging in a culture that equates youth with perfection means waking up every morning one day further removed from that perfection. It means watching something precious vanish before our eyes. Surely, people say, there must be another way -- and they turn to anti-aging gurus and their potions.

Gurus Get Old

No matter how clever, attractive, or entrepreneurial the anti-aging proponents are when they burst on the scene, they immediately begin undermining their own promises. They say they hold the secrets of youth in their hand, but the signs of aging always appear on their faces. If they are blessed with a long life (and not all of them will be), they age greatly. While vitamins, vegetables, and exercise may help keep them spry, such regimens never keep anti-aging gurus young.

Every person who makes a reputation as an anti-aging "guru" sets a karmic retribution into motion. In time, the guru will get old and become wrinkled and gray. Justice delayed may be justice denied, but aging will be neither delayed nor denied.

Anti-aging miracles always fail because they represent a willful denial of our humanity. Anti-aging gurus make, and then profit from, false promises. There is a name for that kind of activity:

Quackery -- Dishonest practices related to claims of special knowledge and skill in some field, typically medicine.

Arnold Ehret was a German naturopath, born in 1866, who believed that white blood cells "poison the blood" and are created as a result of consuming mucus-forming foods.[9] According to Ehret longevity could be assured by cleansing the body of toxins (he developed and marketed the Innerclean Intestinal Laxative) and avoiding mucus-producing foods. Notably, the Federal government investigated Innerclean and found it to be a fraudulent product. Ehret published *The Mucusless Diet Healing*

System in 1922 and died later that year, at the age of 57.

In the mid 1970s, fitness guru Paul Bragg rewrote Ehret's *Mucusless Diet Healing System* and retitled it as *The Bragg Toxicless Diet Body Purification and Healing System*. He also advertised a patent medicine called "Glantex" which he claimed would make people "feel twenty years younger."[10] While many people tell others they are younger than their actual age, Bragg claimed to be 14 years older than he really was. This deception created an illusion of "youthful vigor" that helped support his claims to knowledge about longevity. Although he claimed to be 95, he actually died at the age of 81.

In 1993, Deepak Chopra published *Ageless Body, Timeless Mind: The Quantum Alternative to Growing Old*. In its pages, Chopra argued that "we are not victims of aging, sickness and death. These are part of the scenery, not of the seer, who is immune to any form of change." Chopra went on to claim that "defeating entropy" would create a "land where no one is old." In 2009, he published Reinventing the Body, Resurrecting the Soul: How to Create a New You. This book diagnosed an "estrangement of body and soul" that can be repaired only by "transforming [your body] from a material object to a dynamic, flowing process."

Surely the author of books promising readers an "ageless body and timeless mind" would himself be "ageless." In the years since his first anti-aging book was published, Chopra has aged in all the ways we would naturally expect. Twenty-five years later, the guru looks 25 years older. While Chopra's mind dreamed of conquering aging, his body revealed the truth

-- aging is normal, and inevitable. Ecstatic promises of "ageless bodies" and "quantum healing" are, and will remain, quackery.

As of 2021, the Chopra Center website carried information on the longevity-inducing properties of the diet championed by Paul Bragg. Recall that Bragg updated Arnold Ehret's unfounded ideas about the role mucus-producing foods supposedly play in health and longevity. Ehret published his book in 1922. A century after Ehret's death, his quackery remains in circulation. Anti-aging gurus get old (and die) but their unfulfilled promises endure.

Aging is reality. Anti-aging is a dream that never dies.

It is tempting to mock the fearfulness that fuels the feverish interest in vitamins, minerals, and "ancient healing herbs" that promise to protect our youth. But we all have certain beliefs that we wish were true, even when we know they aren't. The anti-aging quacks seem to be promoting diet secrets but are actually peddling permission to believe that we still have an unlimited amount of time left to live. This bait and switch helps explain why they rarely market their products to genuinely old people (who would seem to need them most) and instead focus on provoking anxiety in the minds of relatively young people.

The fantasy of indefinite life extension restores and strengthens a devotion to doing, having, and getting that has long been associated with youth and the young.

People who are willing to do anything to stay young are poor candidates for exploring the experience of normal human aging. Quacks and quackery lead us away from the common sense things we can do to improve and enrich our lives as we grow older. After all, why should we bother working out new ways to move, eat, sleep and heal if all we have to do to stay young is to "transform our bodies from material objects into a dynamic, flowing process."

Anti-aging gurus promise to turn old people into young people -- and always fail.

MESH promises to turn old people into old people with greater strength, purpose and belonging -- and often succeeds.

Fountains of Age

Modern society has placed the crown jewel of longevity in the hands of millions of people while at the same time draining old age of its spirit, worth, and depth. This is not unlike a host who lays out a feast for the guests and then pretends the food is spoiled and the wine has gone rancid. Everyone sits before an appetizing banquet, their hands folded in their laps, not daring to eat or drink.

Put another way, our preoccupation with productive adulthood keeps people away from the richness of aging in much the same way that medieval mapmakers warned travelers away from the edge of a supposedly flat earth. Convinced that those who strayed too far from familiar terrain were bound to perish, the far limits of their maps included the warning:

"There be dragons here." We now know that the world is round and that dragons are figments of superstitious imaginations. Old age, however, remains a fearful realm.

Given these cultural preoccupations, it is no surprise that adults tend to scare themselves with fearful interpretations of what they suppose old age will be like. We tremble before the loss of function that defines the edge of our social world. For many, getting old is a calamity, nearly as fearsome as death itself. In trembling whispers we are told that to "give in" to old age is to court banishment from our accustomed place in society. This is nonsense. Every age arrives with its own burdens and blessings, old age included.

Fountains of youth are just another species of ageist propaganda, with no practical purpose. The young are already young. The old have likely outgrown fairy tales. Discovering a fountain of age would be much more useful. In 1993, Betty Friedan described how struggling to hold on to the illusion of youth denies reality and evades the triumphs associated with growing older. She concluded, "I have discovered that there is a crucial difference between society's image of old people and 'us' as we know and feel ourselves to be." We drink from the Fountain of Age when we value how we "know and feel ourselves to be" over and above "society's image of old people."[11]

Anti-aging advocates seek strength and beauty because they want to act like, and be seen as, young people. Instead of searching the world for magic water, elders seek insights that can help them continue their journey through life.

It is the simple things, done well, that endow us with strength, purpose and belonging in old age.

The fountain of age is right in front of us. It is ready to show us how to move, eat, sleep and heal, as we grow old.

Move

Living things move.

Plants move. Botanist Roger Hangarter observes that, "Compared to the relatively hyperactive activities of humans, plants do not appear to do much but they are actually in constant motion as they develop, respond to environmental stimuli, search for light and nutrients, avoid predators, exploit neighbors, and reproduce."[12]

Animals move. Scientists placed a GPS tracker on a gray wolf from Mongolia and found that it covered 4,503 miles in a single year.[13] A tagged bar-tailed godwit currently holds the record for nonstop avian migration, flying 7,500 miles non-stop from Alaska to New Zealand in just eleven days.[14]

People Move. Before we take our first breath right up until we take our last -- we move.

Some people experience the need to move more acutely than others. The first man to complete a verified "walk around the world" is Dave Kunst. "Over the course of four years, three months, and sixteen days, Kunst travelled across thirteen countries by foot, including the U.S., Portugal, India, Afghanistan, and Australia."[15] He walked 14,450 miles, wore out 21 pairs of shoes, and found the love of his life. The first time long distance swimmer Diana Nyad attempted to swim from Cuba to Key West, she was 28 years old. She fell short and tried again, and again, and again. Diana succeeded on her fifth attempt, covering 110 shark-infested miles in 53 hours. She was 64 years old at the time.[16]

The thing is that, while we all need to move, very few of us are like Dave and Diana, and that is all right. No one needs to aim for a world record but not moving is a serious problem.

Our bodies are made to move every day and not moving leads directly to "de-conditioning." What most people call "couch potato syndrome" is actually a complex set of psychological and physiological changes that follow in the wake of inactivity, bedrest or a sedentary lifestyle.

Research shows us that when old people are hospitalized, the experience is associated with diminished muscle strength ranging from two to five percent per hospital-day, and the development of serious limitations in mobility and joint range of motion. Not surprisingly, these changes are also linked to post-hospitalization falls, functional decline, increased frailty, and immobility.

Worldwide, around 3.2 million deaths per year can be attributed to inactivity. In countries with greater longevity, the prevalence of chronic health conditions is increasing and levels of physical activity are declining.[17] The phenomenon of de-conditioning requires significant effort to reverse. In this case, an ounce of prevention is worth ten pounds of cure.

People need to move if they are to remain healthy and people who are sick or injured need to move if they are to get well.

This dictum applies to people of all ages and conditions but it is especially relevant to old people.

Poise

Poise consists of a delicious blend of posture and balance. All of us have poise and it feels so natural to us, so ordinary, so reliable, that we rarely stop to think of the complex interactions that connect its twin elements. Amazing things start to happen when we begin to give posture and balance the attention they so richly deserve. We gain poise.

For most people, just reading the word "posture" causes them to sit up a little straighter in their chair. Shoulders back. Stomach in. Chest out. They hear a grandmotherly voice admonishing them: "Stand straight! Don't slouch!" and remember being warned that bad posture leads to bad character. Posture actually has nothing to do with morals, but is important to our health and well-being.

The idea that there are very particular ways that we should, and should not, stand, sit, or move is a fairly recent invention that sprang from a surprising source. Posture got its start as a military technology. As muskets became more common in European armies, soldiers were drilled in assuming the correct posture for the use of these weapons. Better posture yielded better aim. By the 18th century, it became clear that posture could also be used to enforce discipline and enhance conformity.[18]

Soldiers were taught to stand "at attention."

- Arms fixed at the side, thumb or middle finger parallel to trouser or skirt seam.
- Head and eyes locked in a fixed forward posture. Eyes unmoving. Blank facial expression.
- Heels together, toes apart,

with the feet at a 45 degree angle.

In the 1700's, the utility of posture as an instrument of control attracted the attention of actor Tiberio Fiorillo who left his native Naples and found fame and fortune as a "posture expert" teaching comportment to London's fashion-minded elite.[19] Observing this trend toward affected posture, Samuel Johnson, who never missed an opportunity to deflate puffery, described a posture expert as "one who teaches or practices artificial contortions of the body."[20] By the middle of the 19th Century, however, posture had emerged as a society-wide concern and the "line between [posture] and moral position became blurred."[21]

From there it was a short hop to posture as a medical matter. A posture craze gripped the American public in the late 19th century (similar to the jogging craze that occurred a hundred years later) and, in 1890, half of all children were identified as having 'abnormal' spinal curvatures. The American Posture League was founded in 1914 by educator Jessie H. Bancroft, and Henry Ling Taylor, an orthopedic surgeon.[22] The League used their research on posture to make recommendations to manufacturers of footwear, furniture, and clothing and it charged fees for the use of "Posture League" labels. The Baby Boomers, however, showed little interest in the Posture League's many admonitions. Indeed, Joan Didion's famous essay on the hippies of San Francisco was titled, "Slouching Toward Bethlehem." Everyone knew what she meant.

Regardless of what people may believe about posture, gravity and time do have their own designs on us. It is true that, with time, people's posture begins to change. Many people find that their heads begin to tip slightly forward, then their shoulders follow suit. This accounts for a "stooped appearance." Sometimes these changes are due to unavoidable complications related to medical conditions. Much more often, the change is the result of a gradual shift in our core muscles. What looks like a spine problem is often actually a muscle problem.[23]

Posture is something we can feel and a good way to get the feel of good posture is to:

1. **Stand against a wall with your head, shoulders, hips, and feet touching the wall.**
2. **Move your arms up and down against the wall ten times, as if you were making a snow angel.**
3. **Walk away, and feel how your body is aligned.**

If your body feels different from the usual you may be able to create better alignment using simple insights and exercises.

When our heads are in "neutral position" our ears line up with our shoulders. A "forward head posture" is defined by a head that tilts slightly toward the chest with the ears assuming a position in front of the body's vertical midline. People of all ages are currently contending with an epidemic of forward head posture due mainly to the fact that we spend so much of our time looking down at our phones and notebook computers.

Some people begin to carry their shoulders and even their upper back forward of the body's vertical midline. This is called "kyphosis." The most common form of this condition is called "postural kyphosis" and it occurs in people of all ages.[24] Not surprisingly, a condition that results from developing a bad posture can very often be improved by cultivating a good posture. Kyphosis can often be cured by working to increase flexibility in the upper back while strengthening the extensor muscles between the shoulder blades.

Good posture is important and not because it helps a person aim a musket accurately, or because it demonstrates moral rectitude. It matters because it centers our weight near the body's vertical axis and that makes it easier to maintain our balance. Balance and posture are closely connected and how we move depends greatly on how we tend to hold ourselves when we are not moving.

What we call **"balance"** is the product of a delicate interplay between three sensory systems and a brain that is capable of weaving them together.

- We use our vision to locate us in three dimensional space. Our eyes tell us what's up and down, left and right.
- Our body also contains sensors that give us information about where our arms, legs, head,

and trunk are located. This is called proprioception.

- Our auditory system also contains a vestibular organ that detects even the smallest movements of our head.
- Our brain pieces this information together and sends signals to our muscles so they can act to maintain our position.

People can improve their balance by understanding how each of these systems work and then "working around" their own particular balance weak spots. For example, a person living with damage to their vestibular system can compensate by working to improve the visual and proprioceptive input their brain receives. Another person might have all three sensory systems working perfectly but feel unsteady because a medication they are taking is interfering with the brain's ability to integrate the information it receives. The point is that taking a balanced approach to balance can yield significant improvements over time. To a degree far greater than is commonly understood -- our balance is under our control.

Although posture and balance are often addressed separately, it is better to tackle them at the same time. Doing so puts us on the path to poise. If girls in 18th century London could study under a "posture expert," old people living in the 21st century ought to be able to study under a "poise coach." Why not work to improve posture when doing so can prevent, or reverse, forward head posture and kyphosis? Why shouldn't we seek out and begin to understand our own unique balance challenges? Doing these things can help us move more freely and easily. Combining these two efforts can make a major difference in the quality of people's lives.

Ballet dancers cultivate poise so they can use its precise beauty in their performances. Old people should follow their example and learn to sit, stand, and move with newfound grace and beauty. Imagine a community of old people led by and inspired by a skilled Poise Coach. See them working together to help each other improve their posture and enrich their shared understanding of balance. The elders living in such a community would look different, even to the most casual observer. People could see, and admire, the command of posture and balance and hope that, when they are old, they too might be blessed with poise.

Because poise forms the foundation for all of the body's movements, people who lose their poise can become reluctant to take risks, afraid to expose themselves to criticism and, finally, reluctant to make the efforts needed to restore their poise.

This self censoring behavior creates a downward spiral of immobility, deconditioning, worsening posture and less reliable balance. Gradually, they withdraw from society and many descend into social isolation and loneliness. It does not have to be this way. We may not be able to cure cancer but we can improve our poise -- if we choose to do so.

Keeping a human body upright and moving is a spectacular feat of coordination and reaction under any circumstances. Doing so in the later decade of life is even more remarkable. Moving with poise is, and will always be, beautiful.

Grip

The palmar grasp reflex appears at about 16 weeks of gestation. After we are born, this primitive reflex thrills parents and siblings as the baby grips and then "holds" their fingers. Learning to grip, grasp, twist, turn and hold objects is a major focus of every child's development.

We must all learn how to grip in order to use eating utensils, pencils, bats, balls, and keys. In time, we grasp our independence.

As we age, our ability to continue living independently depends greatly on maintaining our ability to grip and grasp objects we encounter on a daily basis. Grip strength also emerges as an indicator of overall health status. People who retain higher levels of grip strength throughout life have been shown to have a reduced risk of several common, life-threatening diseases.

A study published in the British Medical Journal examined the grip strength of half a million adults between the ages of 40 and 69. They correlated these findings with data about the participants' history of heart disease, respiratory disease or cancer and adjusted for diet, sedentary time and socioeconomic status. The data showed that reduced grip strength was associated with an elevated risk of heart disease, lung disease, cancer, and was associated with reduced cognitive function.[25] Findings from studies on grip strength have also shown that:

- Men in their 20's have the highest grip strength, 101 pounds on average.
- Women in their 20's have an average of 64 pounds of grip

strength.

- Men in their 60's have an average of 69 pounds of grip strength.
- Women in their 60's have an average of 52 pounds of grip strength.
- Women over the age of 75 have the lowest grip strength on average.
- A grip-strength measurement of less than 57 pounds for men and less than 35 pounds for women is associated with "higher overall risk of death and higher risk for specific illnesses."

What is your grip strength?

Typically, grip strength is measured using a dynamometer. The person being tested holds the device as if it was a glass of water, with their elbow close to their side and the elbow at a 90 degree angle. A common practice is to ask the person to squeeze the dynamometer as hard as they can for five seconds. The test is performed on both hands, usually allowing three attempts on each hand. Finally, an average is taken of all attempts. This is our grip strength.

Normal aging results in a gradual loss of muscle mass, about one percent a year starting in the 30’s. Loss of muscle tissue also occurs as a consequence of specific health conditions. Our hands can give us a useful, easy to access, measure of strength and overall health.

Getting serious about grip strength can also help us help others protect and extend their independence. Having a stronger grip is also associated with greater health, well-being, and longevity. Grip strength is closely correlated with total body muscle mass and improvements in grip strength are associated with greater skeletal muscle mass.

Our hands, and especially our thumbs and fingers, are our main contact points with the world.

According to the Social Security Administration a person who loses all the toes on one foot is thought to be 20 percent disabled. A person who loses all the fingers on one hand is considered to be 60 percent disabled.26 No matter the cause, the loss of grip strength can also be disabling in significant ways. In fact, below a minimum level of grip strength it is very difficult to maintain one's independence.

We use the phrase "get a grip" to mean keeping or recovering one's self-control. It ought to also refer to getting serious about grip strength and understanding the different grips we use in daily life.

- The **"crush grip"** is the one we use when we are shaking hands, or evaluating our core grip strength.
- The **"support grip"** is used when we carry a bale of hay, a suitcase, or a bag of groceries.
- The **"pinch grip"** occurs when we bring the thumb and fingertips together.

Experts have identified five different types of pinch grip and it is useful to understand each type. [27]

- **Pinch of Salt Grip:** The thumb tip to fingertip grip is what we use when we pick up a pinch of salt. This is also called the two-point tip pinch.
- **Ballpoint Pen Grip:** The tip of the thumb meets with the tips

of the forefinger and middle finger, as when holding a pen. This is also known as the three-point tip pinch.

- **Light Bulb Grip:** The thumb and the pad of the index finger are used to maneuver objects such as a light bulb. This is known as the two-point pad pinch.
- **The Bottle Cap Grip:** The thumb opposes the fingers such as when unscrewing a bottle cap. This is sometimes referred to as the three-point pad pinch.
- **The House Key Grip:** A thin object is held between the lateral surface of the index finger and the thumb, such as when using a key. This is also called the lateral pinch.

A human hand contains 27 bones, 27 joints, 34 muscles, and

over 100 ligaments and tendons. Grip training regimens focus on delivering improvements in three areas.

1. We can improve the **flexibility** of every one of those 27 joints.
2. We can increase the **strength** of each of our 34 muscles.
3. We can build **stamina** when using 8 kinds of grip.

There is no reason that people who have some use of their hands can not increase their grip strength. We have reason to believe that doing things that improve grip strength also leads to greater total strength. This is important because even small changes in the strength of our grip (and our total muscle mass) can yield big benefits in terms of our ability to live where and how we choose.

What if?

What if there was a community of elders who had regular access to a "Hand Gym." The exercise equipment would be quite small compared to a big gym designed for big muscles. But the impact would be large.

The Hand Gym would come complete with a "Grip Coach," a person who understood the importance of hands and how to make them stronger and more flexible. Working with the Grip Coach the elders of this community would begin to see changes in their lives. A weak handshake would give way to a hearty handshake. A key that always gave them trouble would turn easily in its lock. Jars and bottles would surrender their lids to their mighty grips.

These elders would be less likely to be admitted to the hospital and would likely live more independently for longer. Sometimes little things make a big difference.

Stamina

In the 1950s, research showed America's youth were out of shape and in poor health compared with their counterparts in Europe. When President Kennedy took office, he made improving the nation's fitness a top priority but it was Lyndon Johnson who launched the Presidential Fitness Challenge in 1966. "The designers chose challenges to mimic the physical prowess that young Americans would need to serve in the military. For example, kids had to throw a softball to show they could theoretically throw a grenade."[28]

If a student placed in the top 15th percentile in every category, they received the Presidential Fitness Award. It should be noted that most students -- did not get the award. For example...

"So I was partnered with the girl I'd had a crush on for like two years for the sit-up portion. She did hers first, and did like 75. I went next, and did around 20, I was tomato-red in the face, sweating buckets, and panting like a dog in a sauna. My partner asked me, 'Do you have asthma?' to which I managed to stammer out a 'No.' She then looked me straight in the eyes and said, 'Wow. Ummm, you might need to lay off the burritos and run some, okay?' Not exactly the outcome I was hoping for."[29]

In 2009 Rita Arens set out to write an article about the test, "I started out with every intention of writing about kids and the Presidential Physical Fitness Test, but what I found was a whole bunch of adults with post-traumatic stress about the test." It turns out that creating a single standard for "fitness" is a recipe for broken dreams.

Designing a fitness test for young people should have been a straightforward exercise because young people are, generally, quite similar to others their age. For example, four-year-olds are almost all around 40 inches tall and usually weigh about 40 pounds.

Making a test for physical fitness that could be applied to all school aged-children should have been easy. It was actually devilishly difficult. Thinking about measuring the fitness of people in their eighties is vastly more challenging. There is a fancy term that is used to refer to a principle that is as common as a high school reunion: "age-related polymorphism." This term refers to the fact that the people who went to high school together become more different from each other the older they get. A fiftieth high school reunion is a great place to see age-related polymorphism in action. The people gathered there display a wide range of physical and mental capabilities. Certainly, there is no single standard of fitness that can be applied to them. Instead, we have to ask, "For what purpose do old people need to be fit?"

NASA sets a standard of fitness for the people they shoot into space on rockets. Few 80 year olds meet those standards, but is that not a problem because few 80 year olds venture into space. What people really need is to be fit enough to live the life they choose. People who are 80 years old and want to keep living in a fifth floor walkup need to be able to go up and down those stairs. An 80 year old person living on the fifth floor of a building with an elevator needs to be fit enough to walk on level surfaces. Different people, different situations, different levels of stamina.

Now for the hard part.

An 80 year old with the energy and drive of a 40 year old is not actually a healthy person. All that energy makes them act and feel very youthful but youthfulness belongs to the young. We can see the problems an abundance of stamina can create when we look at elite professional athletes. The few among them who are blessed with a long career can begin to feel that being aggressive, strong and fast is the only way to live. Time marches on and these old pros can get lost in life and never outgrow the self-image of a star athlete. At dinner with his wife one evening a world class athlete complained bitterly that he was no longer able to run as fast or jump as high as he used to. His wife listened patiently and then observed, "That's true but you are a much nicer person than you used to be." Excessively high levels of stamina can block an old person's development and lead to the perpetuation of adultish behaviors long after they are useful, or attractive.

Fortunately, having an excess of stamina is a rare affliction. Far more people report not having the energy and drive they need to live the life they have chosen. One way to fix this problem is to adjust our expectations to match our experiences. A person who believes, "I can't be happy if I don't play tennis three times a week," yet is in a lot of pain when they do so can examine the 'why' behind this belief. Why would tennis three times a week make them happy? Is it the routine and ritual? If so, they can ask themselves "Would I be happier playing tennis three times a week at a pace that feels better on my body?" If yes, they can change their expectation to "I'll be happy if I get on the court three times a week and listen to my body" or maybe challenging their body is part of their 'why' and they will decide to change their expectation to "I will be happy if I play tennis once a week and push myself to my physical edge and then recover the rest of the week." After all, there is no law that says that a person must play tennis three times a week. Adjusting expectations can be difficult but also offers immediate rewards in terms of greater fitness, along with less self-doubt and worry.

We decide how fit we need to be and it is foolish to insist that maximum stamina is the only option on the table. Our fitness level should match the life we have chosen to live.

Youthful preoccupations create the illusion that stamina is the product of a relentless struggle against lethargy. Old people often report being "so busy that I don't know how I ever had time for work." Busy! Busy!

Busy! Always going, going, going! This kind of language is reassuring to the speaker and somewhat off putting to the listener. We get it, you are that bunny that belongs to that battery company, good for you. Here is what those bunnies fail to understand.

Getting serious about building our stamina also requires us to get serious about rest and recovery.

The older we get, the more important it is to manage rest and recovery skillfully. A pioneer in the field of aging (and one of the two people this book is dedicated to) made it a habit to take a nap everyday in the early afternoon. Although she was often surrounded by energized young people, she knew better than to try to keep up with them. She also knew that she could lead by example and teach those young people that her afternoon siesta was both valuable and important. Cultivating a talent for restful relaxation offers us the widest, smoothest path to greater stamina.

The approach to stamina favored by most young people is based on maximum effort.

Youth understands full well that our bodies are equipped with the ability to reshape themselves to meet the demands we place on them. Most young people know how to "get into shape" and can do so very quickly. A decision is made and soon there are workout clothes (and sometimes a gym membership). As the sweat beads on their foreheads their bodies get the message, it's time for a change.

All of this is true for old people as well but, in their case, the exertion needs to ramp up more slowly and smoothly. There needs to be plenty of scheduled time for rest and restoration, and expectations need to be kept in line with reality. One of the first signs of aging generally recognized by younger people occurs when they begin to understand that sudden intermittent physical exertion doesn't yield the results it used to and may lead to a visit to the urgent care center. Old people know better than to play soccer with teenagers.

Simple Things That Should Be Remembered.

- Decide how fit you need to be to live the life you want. Our bodies are designed to match our fitness to our level of activity and it is very hard to fool them. If you want to have more muscle and bone you must live a life that requires more muscle and bone.
- Remember that adjusting

expectations is the fastest way to achieve optimum fitness. Setting expectations too high, too fast can lead to discouragement and even the loss of progress.

- Rest and Recovery are essential tools and need to be an important part of your plan.
- When you decide to challenge your body do so in a slow, smooth, gradual way.

**You can also eat Wheaties, if you want to.*

Falling

Saturday

Philip Asdair Montgomery was widely known for his remarkable ability to fall in love. Married six times, divorced four times and widowed twice, he'd loved and lost more than most people. Always a natty dresser, Philip (never Phil) kept a fine garden, doted on his daughters and babied his heirloom tomatoes. He also insisted that clean gutters went hand in hand with clean living and it was this uncompromising commitment to gutter hygiene that proved to be his undoing.

Even though he was 90 years old, even though his girls had pleaded with him not to do it, Philip leaned a ladder against the back of the house on a sunny summer morning. He double-checked its footing and went to work. Front, back and side downspouts checked, the gutters were clean and all was right in the world. Sweat beaded his forehead as he carefully descended the ladder one rung at a time. He felt for the bottom rung with his foot but slipped, and he lost his grip on the upper rung. He stumbled and fell to the ground.

He cursed a blue streak then sat up and checked himself over. His right wrist was a little sore. Not too bad, he thought, for a fellow my age. Eight hours later, however, the wrist was throbbing. It had ballooned to twice its usual size and the skin was shiny and bright red. Something was wrong.

He drove himself to the hospital and, after three hours in the waiting area, saw a doctor. X-rays were ordered and, after another long wait, the doctor confirmed Phillip's suspicion. "It's broken. Just a crack but you'll need a cast when the swelling goes down." After being fitted with a wrist splint, Philip was handed a sheaf of papers including prescriptions and discharge instructions. He would need to make an appointment with the on-call orthopedist. As he was wheeled to the door he got a stern lecture on acting his age: "90-year-olds and ladders don't mix." Philip rolled his eyes. In the parking lot he fumbled with the key fob; it was the first time he had used it with his left hand.

Tuesday

Three days later, everything was worse. He'd taken his medicine and iced his wrist as instructed but he didn't think he could wait another week for his appointment. The pills upset his stomach and he felt "weak as a baby." His right hand was swollen, discolored and hurt like hell, and

Philip, who usually "slept like a stone" was up all night.

Wednesday

In the morning his neighbor stopped by to check on him and it was obvious Phillip hadn't shaved or showered. He appeared confused so she called 911 and a dispatcher sent an ambulance to the house.

This time, instead of making snappy conversation with the nurses, Phillip mumbled answers to their questions. An orthopedic nurse practitioner examined him and noted that it did not appear that he had been using "the sling he was sent home with." She also observed that the patient "appears quite drowsy." But, because she had never seen Philip before, and assumed this type of appearance was normal for a 90-year-old man, she made nothing of it. The X-rays were repeated and they, at least, showed no change. Philip's chief complaint was "pain and swelling" so the narcotic pain medication was doubled and a stronger non-steroidal anti-inflammatory was added to the mix.

A nurse fitted him with a new sling and a sturdier splint. As they wheeled him to the door he repeated the mantra to a bleary Philip Asdair Montgomery:

- Ice.
- Elevation.
- Take your medications.
- Follow-up with the orthopedist.

The Emergency Department's job was done.

Friday

At lunchtime, the same neighbor noticed that Philip hadn't gotten his mail so she came over. She found him on the floor of the bathroom — trousers bunched around his ankles.

She called 911, again. Again, an ambulance took him to the emergency department. This time, Philip was lethargic and had difficulty understanding where he was or what was happening. The ER was also very busy and Philip's stretcher was parked in a hallway for several hours. When the department's ceaseless clamor did arouse him, he was overcome with a jumble of memories from his time in the Navy.

His daughters arrived from out of town and barely recognized their father. Nor did he recognize them. He thrashed against the stretcher's side rails hallucinating and calling for help. His daughters hovered, anxious and afraid. After a six hour wait, Philip Asdair Montgomery was admitted to an orthopedic floor with the diagnoses of right wrist fracture, dehydration and delirium.

Phillip actually fell twice. The first fall followed his foot slipping on the bottom rung of the ladder. The resulting injury was minor (this type of fracture usually heals completely) and the fracture was attended to properly. The second fall was a collapse in his ability to function independently in the world. This fall was the consequence of a health care system that focuses on diagnoses (non-displaced fracture of right wrist) and shows little concern for the person with the fracture. Both of these falls require our attention.

Slips and Trips

Slips and trips are two different things.

Slips - are the result of too little friction between footwear and surface.

Trips - happen when the foot strikes an object unexpectedly and causes a sudden loss of balance.

Most people who trip fall forward. Most people who slip fall backward. Not all slips and trips lead to falls, we have all "caught ourselves" and stopped a fall from happening.

The ability to catch ourselves depends on:

- **Poise**
- **Grip Strength**
- **Stamina**

During his first ER visit, a nurse told Phillip that "90-year-olds and ladders don't mix." This is both wrong and ageist. The truth is that people with unsteady balance, diminished grip strength and limited stamina and ladders don't mix.

Age doesn't matter but ability sure does.

A 90 year old man who wishes to keep climbing ladders must assess and manage his balance and strength because these assets are essential to that kind of movement. We know from personal experience that the difference between falling and not falling is often very small. This helps explain why even small changes in strength and balance can actually make a big difference -- in a good way. That's important because falls often make a big difference -- in a bad way.

Every 13 seconds an old person is treated in an emergency room for injuries related to a fall; every 20 minutes, an old person dies from such injuries.

Falls are the leading cause of fatal injury and the most common cause of nonfatal trauma-related hospital admissions among older adults.[30] Many people who fall, even if they aren't injured, develop a fear of falling that may cause them to limit their activities, which in turn leads to reduced mobility and loss of physical fitness. As fitness declines, the likelihood of falls rises.[31]

Falls are a nasty business so it is no surprise that people have become interested in the idea of "fall proofing." Reducing the risk of slips and trips by evaluating and modifying home environments is important and can make homes safer for their inhabitants but it is also important to help people fall proof themselves. As we have seen, we can all make changes in our posture, balance, grip strength and stamina that make it less likely that a slip or trip will lead to a fall. Beyond that, learning how to fall as safely as possible and how to react after a fall can change people's lives for the better.

Falling into a Gap in Care

The Office of Inspector General, the Department of Health and Human Services, and the Institute of Medicine have all issued reports concluding that the acute care system is failing America's elders. The inclusion of the word "system" in the term "health care system" is, frankly, a matter of false advertising. As experienced daily by elders and their families, health care consists of scattered clusters of campuses, facilities, insurance programs, and levels of care. The outcomes produced by these clusters are deeply disturbing.

- One in seven Medicare beneficiaries suffers an adverse event during a hospital stay.

- One in five patients discharged from the hospital to home has experienced an adverse inpatient event.

- Patients experiencing delayed transfers from the Emergency Department to ICU (Intensive Care Unit) experience increased hospital length of stay and higher ICU and hospital mortality.

- Delirium complicates hospital stays for at least 20 percent of patients over 65 with potential long-term consequences.

Phillip fell about 12 inches from the bottom rung of his ladder. His fall into the gap in care between the ER and the orthopedic surgeon's office was more like falling off the roof. A broken wrist turned into a life shattering event because the system treated a cracked radius bone but gave little thought to Philip Asdair Montgomery.

Eat

Two doctors, old friends, met one day. It had been a while since they had seen each other and they took time to catch up. Then the older of the two said that his lymphoma had returned after a long absence. They talked about the chemo he was using, then the older doctor paused and said, "I've lost about 15 pounds and I can't seem to put it back on. Nothing tastes good to me anymore." He was speaking in a code they both understood. He was saying: "This is going to be my last fight. I likely won't see you again." The younger doctor nodded and the conversation took a different turn. When they parted they said goodbye, for the last time.

Hunger and Thirst

For most of our lives hunger and thirst guide us with superb simplicity. Hunger is the body's way of telling us to find and eat the foods we need to meet our minimal energy needs.

Thirst pushes people to meet their minimal hydration needs. Thirst is a powerful sensation, but there is little or no consequence for drinking too much water.

Hunger is weaker than thirst but there are significant consequences for eating too much food.[32] But what happens when we can't satisfy our hunger or slake our thirst? Or, even worse, what happens when hunger and thirst quit on the job? That is when things get -- complicated.

Dr. John Morley was the first to define a syndrome he called "anorexia of aging." The word anorexia comes from the Greek 'an' meaning without and 'orexis' meaning appetite. Anorexia of Aging is distinct from its counterpart Anorexia Nervosa which is a psychological condition causing an obsession with one's weight and food intake.

Later studies found that between 15 and 30 percent of old people experience a significant loss of appetite. The rates of anorexia of aging are higher in women, nursing home residents, hospitalized people, and the very old people.[33] Old people with anorexia (loss of appetite) show a decrease in walking speed, decreased hand grip strength, and the loss of function that can impair independence.

As we age, our appetite, along with our daily food consumption, declines. The change is connected to an age-related decrease in energy expenditure. Most old people naturally do less and eat less than young people. What is not natural is the way hospitals nourish older people who are acutely unwell. Older hospital patients are routinely underfed and, far too often, not fed at all.

In one study, a fifth of hospitalized patients 65 years of age or older took in an average nutrient intake of less than half of their calculated maintenance energy requirements. Another study of acute care patients showed that forty percent of the food being served to them was wasted. Imagine the outcry if forty percent of the medications prescribed were tossed into the dumpster. Wherever they may be, old people need access to food and drink in the right form, with the right flavors, with the right assistance and in the right company if they are to avoid the complications caused by under-nutrition.

To return to health and wellness, people need free access to healthful food and drink, when, where and how they want it.

Most parents have heard advice along the lines of, "Don't worry! They'll eat when they're hungry!" One parent of a particularly picky eater put it this way, "[The experts] all explain it the same. 'You cook the food, and if your child doesn't eat, don't worry, he won't starve.' 'Give him what you eat, if he doesn't eat it, he doesn't eat anything at all till the next meal. No meal, no snacks.' 'He won't starve. When he's hungry, he'll eat.' Um . . . it doesn't work that way in my house. Maybe we won't call it starve, but he certainly isn't eating."[34] What this mother knows, and the professionals she's been talking to evidently do not know, is that hunger is just one factor among many and that it is quite possible to experience hunger but choose not to eat.

Our appetite for food is divided into three components:

- **hunger**
- **satiation**
- **satiety**

We all recognize **hunger** pangs as the sensations that lead us to seek out and consume food.

Satiation is the feeling that leads us to push away from the table and say, "I'm full!"

Satiety is an absence of sensation. We experience satiety when the idea of food and drink rarely even enters our minds.[35] As we grow older, our relationship to hunger and thirst, food and drink gradually begins to change. A gradual decrease in appetite is a normal part of aging and old people tend to use fewer calories per day than when they were young.

People choose to eat or not eat based on a complex web of factors including mood, social expectations, food preferences (and aversions), social setting and rituals, and pleasurable sensations related to sight, hearing, taste, and (especially) smell.

At age seventy an average sized man should consume about 2,000 calories a day. Physically active men need about 2,600 calories a day. Because they have less muscle mass women need between 1,600 and 2,000 calories a day.36 If they can't get the nutrients they need from food, the body takes them from muscle and bone.

The idea that the hunger signal alone is enough to ensure good nutrition is a damaging myth that is born out of ignorance and any approach to diet and nutrition that relies on old people getting hungry and deciding to eat is doomed to generate an excess of malnutrition, frailty and death. Studies of people over 65 who live in the community reveal that anorexia and unintentional weight loss shorten peoples' lives.[37]

The first notable aging-related sensory change experienced by most people is "presbyopia" which translates as "old age vision." Print on the screen, or on paper, gets harder to read close up and the changes keep coming until the person gets a pair of "readers" and suddenly appreciates their ability to make reading easy again. When it comes to food, the most important sensory changes are related to the sense of smell. The number of working olfactory glands available for duty diminishes with time and so does the acuity of our sense or smell.

It is estimated that about 80 percent of what we experience as taste is actually derived from the smell of the food we are eating. Researchers recently tracked the health of thousands of people who lost their sense of smell and/or taste as a result of COVID-19. About 40 percent completely regained their sense of smell six months later. Unfortunately, two percent of those enrolled in the study showed no improvement.

Living without a sense of smell can be very difficult. One patient who lost the sense of smell as the result of chemotherapy reported that, "When I'd eat food, I remembered what it was supposed to taste like, but it was a total illusion," he said.

"Eating became something I had to do because I needed to, not because it was an enjoyable experience."[38]

The food put before old people, like all good food, should be aromatic. The aroma should be easy to enjoy and ought to remind them of food they know and love.

Studies have shown that the areas of the brain that process taste and smell are closely linked with areas that host memories of people and places. Some of these memories go back to the earliest years of our lives and are also connected to strong emotions.

Good smells, good memories, and good food go together.

Imagine for a moment the challenge of enjoying a meal that consists of food you don't know (or like) that is served cold and tastes like mush. Now imagine this being true for every meal you eat.

It is important to ask anyone who is experiencing a loss of appetite what medications they are taking. Some of the drugs taken most frequently by old people have also been shown to impair appetite. Also, combinations of medications can lead to anorexia even when none of the drugs (if taken alone) are known to interfere with good nutrition. While a comprehensive medication review can only be completed by a trained clinical professional (doctors, nurses, and pharmacists are able to do this), anyone can ask the question and get the medication evaluation ball rolling. It is also useful to ask for a medical evaluation that looks for conditions such as dry mouth, tooth loss, sores in the mouth, gastritis, ulcers, depression, and delirium.

At present, there is no medication approved for the treatment of anorexia of aging. Nutritional supplements can help prevent malnutrition but do nothing to help people restore appetite or the enjoyment of food. The secret here is no secret at all. We have to go beyond "hunger and thirst" and embrace a broader understanding of how aging changes our relationship with food.

We can begin by focusing on getting the right food to the right person for the right reason and in the right amount.

Feast and Famine

Between 1841 and 1851 at least a million Irish peasants died of starvation and another million fled their homes for distant shores. It is commonly held that Ireland continued to export food (mostly to England) during that time and that anger over this injustice fueled the drive to Irish independence. Like most famines, "the Great Hunger" was due partly to crop failure (due in this case to the potato blight) but was made much worse by politics. Absentee landlords had little reason to care about the fate of those who tilled their land.

A similar pattern holds in the current epidemic of hunger among old people. According to the Government Accounting Office (GAO) only ten percent of people who are over age 60, and have difficulties with daily activities, currently receive home-delivered meals. A report issued in 2014 confirms that providing home delivered meals is key to preventing unnecessary institutionalization. All of this is true in a nation where food is, by any definition, plentiful.

We use the word "hunger" but we are mostly talking about a condition known as "food insecurity"[39] Experiencing food insecurity means living with "limited or uncertain availability of nutritionally adequate and safe foods, or limited or uncertain ability to acquire acceptable foods in socially acceptable ways."

Just as in the Potato Famine, the food that is needed exists but the people who need it can't get it, cook it and eat it in quantities sufficient to maintain good health. Many old people live in "food deserts" where people without a car (or the ability to drive a car) have no supermarket within a mile of their homes. Those who can buy food may not be able to prepare it for themselves. Those who can cook may be experiencing medical conditions, including side-effects of medications, that make it difficult to get enough to eat.

Food insecurity and malnutrition among elders are painful social ills. They are also exceptionally expensive. It has been estimated that poor nutritional status among old people results in a tripling of associated health care costs. Even so, the rate of senior hunger grew by 65 percent between 2007 and 2014. Almost unbelievably, about a third of all elders report "trimming the size of their meals, skipping meals completely or buying less nutritious foods because they didn't have enough money for a proper meal."[40] Because going hungry damages our health and well-being, it leads directly to increased spending on medical services that totals over 130 billion dollars a year.[41]

Reacting to case reports of actual starvation among nursing home residents, the federal government established significant penalties for facilities that allow residents to lose weight "unexpectedly." These facilities find that it is a constant struggle to increase the dietary intake of those under their care. Just how challenging a task they have undertaken becomes obvious when you look at how these facilities think about, acquire, prepare, and serve food.

Institutions buy from large commercial food wholesalers and their "groceries" arrive at the loading dock where they are unloaded from the back end of a tractor trailer. At this scale, planning must be done far in advance of preparation and there is little room for spontaneity. Some facilities, like airlines, outsource food production entirely and take delivery of truckloads of prepared dinners that must be reheated before serving. In a down-to-the-minute ballet, this food is rushed to large dining rooms where scores of people await their next meal. It is a never-ending challenge to serve hot food when it is still hot and cold food when it is still cold.

The people involved do their best but the realities of large-scale food service require that the material characteristics of the food, such as viscosity, temperature, volume and calculated nutritional content, become its most important features. The emphasis on consistency and low cost is relentless. When food is reduced to a series of numbers, meals lose their meaning. The lifelong rhythm of good food shared within the circle of family life is absent. This is somewhat understandable; after all, no family could put 600 hot delicious, nutritious meals on the dinner table 365 days a year.

Rethinking Meals

The elements of human survival are simple and few. A person can get along with a couple of thousand calories a day, a liter of water, a sprinkling of vitamins and minerals, and a steady supply of air to breathe. Or can they?

The relationship between people and the food that sustains them begins with the planning that by necessity must precede each meal. Even when we are "grabbing a bite to eat" we know deep down that a "real meal" is a complicated thing. It springs from thoughtful attention to what people like (and don't like) and extends to the loving hands that turn recipes and ingredients into a meal fit to be shared.

Many of us know this to be true based on lifelong experiences eating meals with our families. For others the truth is revealed the first time they encounter industrialized food (in school, in the military, or in prison).

Health care facilities are the canaries in this coal mine, warning us about the assembly-line approach to food that is spreading through our culture.

Institutions may be able to blame their approach to food on their own gigantic size, but the sad fact is that food is being drained of meaning in homes all across the country.

Fewer meals are shared by the whole family and more of the food being eaten is highly processed than ever before. These trends become even more worrisome when we consider how ageism and common misunderstandings about aging complicate this picture.

Studies of healthy older people show that, compared to younger people, they consume smaller meals, eat more slowly, eat fewer snacks between meals and become satiated after eating smaller portions. These changes are, for the most part, the natural consequence of an age-related decrease in energy expenditure. Taken by themselves, they aren't a big deal, and most old people cope with them quite easily.

When an elder, with a diminished appetite, is admitted to a hospital it is likely they will emerge undernourished and nutritionally unprepared for the healing they must do at home. The loss of a spouse, or the emergence of a condition that makes it difficult to buy and prepare food, can also lead to an accelerating downward spiral of poor nutrition, with the loss of muscle mass and stamina leading to an even more impoverished diet.

Famines are almost never due solely to a lack of food-- they are mainly crises of food availability.

So it is in old age. Most old people can get food. Far fewer can plan for, prepare and consume the food they need, day in and day out.

We can fix this by making it simpler to get enough to eat. The simplest, and most compelling, dietary advice currently available was articulated by Michael Pollan. He summarizes his approach in just seven words, "Eat food, not too much, mostly plants." This turns out to be good advice for people of all ages.

When Pollan says "eat food" he means try to avoid eating things your grandmother wouldn't recognize as food. He also suggests shopping on the outer edges of your supermarket; that is where the fresh foods tend to be located. He also recommends that people not buy food where they buy gasoline. People living in food deserts may have no choice but to do this but gas station food, while convenient, tends to be both expensive and lacking in nutrients.[42]

For decades, medical professionals made the problem of under-eating worse by prescribing restrictive diets for old people. These diets were rarely based on actual clinical evidence and came and went in much the same way as fad diets. While there are clinical conditions that do require people to adopt dietary restrictions, the much bigger problem is people not getting the fats, proteins, and carbohydrates they need to keep their bodies humming. When a restrictive diet is prescribed it is always a good idea to seek an explanation and ask if this diet's risks may outweigh its benefits.

Eating is a social act, perhaps the most common shared social experience of all.

Eating alone puts one at risk for missing meals and makes it more likely that we will stop cooking. People who dine with others eat more and eat better than people who eat alone. Of course this has long been understood. Food has always tasted better when we share it together. A feast is about much more than just food.

Convivium and Community

For 40 years Harry Starrett manned a teller's window for the National Bank and Trust. Every weekday, without fail, his wife Mabel would have dinner waiting for him when he got home. On Sundays she made pot roast, mashed potatoes and her signature old-fashioned green beans. Harry always cleared the table and washed the dishes.

When Mabel was diagnosed with lung cancer, he was by her side every step of the way. She had always been the social one, the one who scheduled visits with friends and arranged parties. After she was gone, Harry's heart ached from loneliness. Instead of supper with Mabel, or cook-outs with their friends, he ate frozen dinners while watching The Weather Channel. Mabel loved The Weather Channel.

His grim determination broke when the bank president announced that they were merging with a much bigger bank. Harry knew what was coming. The new entity shed thousands of jobs. One of them was his. Weeks that had been passing slowly now crawled by, and on the weekend, time seemed to stand still. Harry floated, hopeless and alone, on an ocean of emptiness.

He ran into an old friend of Mabel's at the Post Office and she suggested that Harry join her bridge club. He didn't know the game and he had never really liked her, but he knocked on her door Thursday at 7:00 p.m., as instructed. The weekly games rotated between players' homes and there was always something to drink and nibble on while they played cards. The games soothed Harry's pain and he slowly grew to love his accidental hobby.

A lifetime spent handling money made Harry into a careful observer and gifted him with a keen memory. In particular, he was fascinated by the intricacies of Max Rebattu's "Dutch Spade" bidding method, which people said was developed while Max was vacationing at the beach. The method used a forcing pass system and was devilishly difficult to master. Within a year, he was a sought-after partner for bridge tournaments and he even began to travel to play at larger events. Life was good.

Slowly, very slowly, Harry began to sense that things were changing, that he was changing. At first it was little things, a trace of forgetfulness that only he would notice. He tried not to think about it but deep inside, he knew. His memory was not what it had been. The first time he lost track of play in a tournament, his partner scowled at him over his cards. Occasional errors became routine and his phone stopped ringing. Competitive players didn't want to play with him anymore. He didn't want to play anymore.

After much delay, and with great trepidation, he went to see his primary care physician and told her of his concerns. A screen for dementia was positive and the workup that followed confirmed the bad news. Harry had dementia, most likely of the Alzheimer's type. Because Mabel and Harry had never had children, he was on his own.

He had never been much of a cook but even reheating dinners got to be too much and most of the time dinner consisted of peanut butter spread on crackers. Harry had always been a thin man (Mabel said it was her job to fatten him up) but when he lost 15 pounds, people knew something was wrong. By the time he'd lost 20 pounds it was decided that he couldn't live alone anymore.

Soon after being admitted to a nursing home he coughed at the lunch table. The next day he was placed on a "mechanical soft diet." He was now a pale gray man living a life defined by pills, mushy meals, tepid baths and Bingo. The staff knew nothing of the 40 years Harry and Mabel made a life of love and laughter. All Harry knows is that he is hungry, hungry for love, hungry for Pot Roast and Old-Fashioned Green Beans.

The Romans had a special term for the particular pleasure that accompanies sharing good food with good people. They called this distinctive experience "convivium."

The word has enjoyed a revival recently. The "slow food" movement (an alternative to fast food) has seized upon it as a way of describing dining experiences that are rich in meaning. Fresh, local ingredients prepared according to distinctive regional recipes are served to people eager to share. They use smell, taste, and texture as a springboard to good conversation and vital relationships.

Good food has always offered people much more than just calories, fat, carbohydrates and protein. At its best, food nourishes us, body and soul. A meal can embody powerful symbols of love and acceptance. The bond between comfort and food, which begins at the breast, is fortified throughout childhood and gains renewed strength in the late decades of life. Properly prepared, the meals we cook and serve to elders should be drenched in memory, ritual, and culture.

The ability to create and maintain convivium demands an appreciation of the long, relaxed meal. Time must be taken because food tastes better when it is soaked in anticipation.

The spirit of convivium calls upon us to linger, to savor, and to draw strength not just from the food we are blessed to eat, but also from the people with whom we are blessed to share our meal.

The Romans feasted together often and were well aware of the social dimensions of eating. Eating is one of those things that humans are meant to do together. What if there was a modern community of elders who made a practice of feasting together? What if they rewrote the rhythm of their daily lives to give each other the best possible shot at getting all of the nutrients they needed while also creating greater strength, purpose and belonging? The first thing to go is the habit of eating just three meals a day.

Changes in appetite, and how we digest our food, suggest that many old people would be better off if they ate five smaller meals each day:

- **Breakfast**
- **Elevenses**
- **Midday Feast**
- **Afternoon Tea**
- **Supper**

The day might begin with something little, just enough to break the fast and get moving. Later in the morning, they'd share "Elevenses," sometimes called "second breakfast." The largest meal of the day would be the Midday Feast. Many of these feasts would be dedicated to a person, recognize an event, or celebrate a shared victory. Whenever possible, a Feast should be founded on a reason to eat and drink that goes beyond mere hunger and thirst. Later in the day there would be a little something to tide them over, the British would call this snack "Afternoon Tea." Finally, supper is served in the early evening hours and is just big enough to satisfy, but not so large as to cause digestive discomfort at night.

Each person should be able to find the combination of food and sociability that suits them best. While we often speak of the relationship between food and old people in terms of dining services, or nutritional counseling, what elders really need is to savor the pleasure that comes from sharing good food in good company. Eating more, smaller, meals a day increases the opportunity for convivium and places less stress on the digestive system.

Sleep

It is a myth that old people need less sleep than middle-aged people. In fact, adults require about the same amount of sleep from their 20s into old age.[43] There are, however, changes in how we sleep as we grow older. Sleep scientists refer to increased sleep fragmentation (waking up during the night), decreased sleep efficiency (spending more time in bed awake rather than sleeping), and phase advance (the tendency to go to bed earlier in the evening and rise earlier in the morning) as normal features of sleep in the latter decades of life.

Sleep Fragmentation: waking up during the night

Decreased Sleep Efficiency: spending more time in bed awake

Phase advance: the tendency to go to bed and rise earlier

Unfortunately, there is an abundance of evidence showing that old people who are hospitalized frequently experience a pathological degree of sleep deprivation that harms their ability to function mentally and physically. According to Dr. Krumholz the sleep deprivation experienced by people who have been hospitalized can adversely affect "metabolism, cognitive performance, physical functioning and coordination, immune function, coagulation cascade, and cardiac risk."[44] These disturbances may confer jet-lag–type disabilities. Studies of people with jet lag have revealed increased incidence of dysphoric mood, diminished physical performance, cognitive impairment, and gastrointestinal disturbances.

The hospital's malign indifference to sleep is so pervasive that discharged patients routinely report being "exhausted" when they leave the hospital and are often desperate for sleep. The 24/7 routine that governs inpatient units shatters the normal circadian rhythm and diminishes natural ability to heal. During the first day after a hospitalization, every effort must be made to create comfort, relieve worry and pain and eliminate distractions -- so that people can sleep.

To return to health and wellness, people need to sleep fully and deeply.

Understanding age-related changes can help us master sleep and cultivate new, better, sleep habits.

From Dream to Nightmare

"Sleep is the golden chain that ties health and our bodies together."
— Thomas Dekker[45]

All animals sleep. They need recovery sleep when they have been awake longer than usual, and suffer serious consequences when they are denied sleep. While the need for sleep is consistent, the amount of sleep required varies widely. Horses can get by on as little as two hours of sleep a day. Some species of bats need almost 20 hours of sleep a day. Left to their own devices, human beings spend a third of our lives sleeping. It has been suggested that predators sleep more (because they have less to fear) and prey sleep less because, well, they are prey -- but this rule has many exceptions. The fact is that no one knows why different animals need different amounts of sleep.

Sleep seems simple. We close our eyes and "drift off." Later, we "wake up" and go about our business, hopefully while feeling rested and refreshed. But the closer we look, the more complicated things become.

We will begin with the simplest, and hardest, question -- What is sleep?

Shakespeare defined sleep as that which soothes our worries and "knits up the raveled sleave of care."[46] Centuries later neuroscientists expanded his definition to include elements of bodily repair that are associated with sleep. A wide range of medical studies have revealed that sleep is essential to all of the body's most important restorative functions.

We grow new muscle while we sleep, we make proteins and repair tissue while asleep. Sleep keeps our immune systems healthy and on track to fight infections. From the outside, a sleeping person looks completely passive but on the inside, sleep fuels the growth and repair of brain tissue at every age.

Doctors define sleep as a natural, recurring state marked by the loss of awareness of one's surroundings accompanied by a typical body posture (such as lying down with the eyes closed). More specifically, our brains cycle through stages of REM (dreaming) and non-REM (deep) sleep. Coma and death resemble sleep in important ways (loss of awareness; cessation of movement) but sleep is, thankfully, easily and rapidly reversible -- and they are not.

Stella knew from the first moment she saw the tidy blue house on the corner of Maple Street and Lake Avenue that she was meant to live there for the rest of her life. Though 63 years had gone by, she still loved her house.

Her husband, Jack, had grumbled that it was too expensive and he might have been right—it was listed for $17,000! Stella could never suppress a smile when, in later years, Jack would brag that his house was the best investment he had ever made.

Together they had raised four children in this house and grieved the loss of their little Amelia. Two generations of neighborhood children had taken lessons from Stella on the piano that still stood in the front parlor. She had given up on the lessons but the house on Maple Street was, and would always be, her home.

Stella liked to wake up slowly, lingering between the covers before starting her day. Jack got up before her and made the coffee. She always said the smell of Jack's coffee was the best alarm clock. After Jack left for work, she made toast with raspberry jam, and had a second cup of coffee. Then came a shower, her makeup, and picking an outfit for the day. By 10:30 AM Stella was ready to tackle the world. And she did. In the evening, Jack would kiss her on the forehead and wander off to bed. She stayed up reading, knitting, puttering around the house doing the little things that needed to be done. It was usually after midnight when sleep finally called to her.

She kept to her routine, even after Jack died.

Then came a morning that was different from all the others. As she drifted toward wakefulness something felt strange. She wiggled her toes under the covers. No problem there. The problem was her right hand — it was clumsy and thick, not at all like the hand of a piano player. She crawled out of bed and shuffled into the bathroom. In the mirror a stranger's face peered back at her. The right side of her face sagged like a wilted flower. Something was terribly wrong. Stella returned to her bedroom and, with difficulty, punched the numbers 9-1-1. The dispatcher answered but Stella found that she could not speak. The dispatcher could hear Stella's panicked breathing and told her to press 4 for yes and 5 for no.

Are you alone?
"4"
Can you speak?
"5"

Do you need an ambulance?
"4"
I'll send one right away.

The EMTs found Stella slumped across her bed. Her only response to their many questions came in the form of a soft moan.

In the emergency department, her oldest daughter, Jean, broke the news. "The doctors say it's a stroke, Mom." In the space of just one morning, her old life was gone. It was dinnertime before Stella was admitted to the medical surgical nursing unit on 3-West.

The staff was friendly and seemed to know what they were doing, but there were so many of them—nurses, nurse aides, doctors of all kinds, along with different types of therapists. There were tests too. So many tests.

Stella was still awake at three in the morning so the nurse called the on-call doctor for a sleeping pill. It made her drowsy and she slept a little. At six in the morning a breakfast tray was delivered, but Stella did not eat. She took short naps during the day but the hospital's night time clamor would not let her sleep, even with the pill.

On the third day they transferred her to inpatient rehabilitation. New nurses, new doctors, new therapists, new roommate, everything was new.

She was hungry but it was hard to eat with her left hand and she still could not speak. Nights and days changed places. She nodded off when she was supposed to be doing therapy and stared at the ceiling most of the night. She was supposed to get stronger. In fact, she was getting weaker.

She got up to use the bathroom in the middle of the night, slipped, and fell backward, striking her head against the toilet. Everyone came running and Stella was transferred to the ICU. She was stabilized and a skilled nurse performed checks on Stella's neurological status every two hours -- round the clock. New medications were added to her regimen. Stella no longer had the energy to communicate with her family or the clinical team. Her blood pressure fell dangerously low. Additional medications were ordered. She stopped eating entirely. Sleep came in scattered fragments.

Stella's children gathered in a cluster for whispered conversations burdened by fear, grief and worry.

After five days in the ICU Stella was ready to be transferred to the medical floor but she no longer knew where she was. After three days on the medical floor she was returned to the inpatient rehabilitation unit. Again, there were new doctors, nurses and therapists. After a week in rehab, it was determined that she was not making progress and that she needed nursing home care.

Stella was transferred from the hospital to the nursing home without a family member in attendance. Jean arrived after work and met with the nursing home social worker. The computer said Stella's name was "Mary" but Jean explained that everyone, even her children, called her Stella. That weekend Tommy put a sign above his mother's bed. "My Name is Stella!" It did not work.

Two days after admission, Stella developed a rash that her daughter recognized as her mother's allergy to laundry soap. She brought clothes and bed linens from home and requested that the staff use them because they had been washed at home. They informed her that it was against policy. The rash got worse and Benadryl was prescribed for the itching. A report filed later concluded that "Chronic sleep deprivation and grogginess caused by the prescribed antihistamine each contributed to the patient's loss of balance and subsequent (second) fall in the bathroom."

Stella did not survive her second fall.

She had been blessed with a happy marriage, loving children, and the ability to live her life according to her body's internal clock. She was a night owl, married to a lark, and they made it work. After her stroke Stella spent the remainder of her days living on facility-time. She was desperate for sleep when she was supposed to be receiving physical therapy, and tormented by insomnia when she was supposed to be asleep. In the end, the lack of sleep made it impossible for her to make progress after her stroke.

The disruption of Stella's normal sleep pattern became a nightmare that hastened her death but the people caring for her made little note of it. Like Stella, everyone who has ever spent time in a healthcare facility learns a bitter truth. Inside those walls, sleep is very hard to come by.

Children of the Gods

"Two households, both alike in dignity..."
-- William Shakespeare, *Romeo and Juliet*

People have long told stories about sleep, and speculated on what happens to us when we are sleeping.

The ancient Greeks worshipped "Hypnos" as the god of sleep. He was the son of Nyx, the goddess of the night, and twin brother to Thanatos, the god of death. His son, Morpehus, served as the god of dreams. Hypnos was highly regarded by the Greeks because of his ability to induce sleep that erased their worldly worries. He was often recruited by other gods to carry out their schemes, wise and unwise.

Once, Selene, the goddess of the Moon, fell in love with a mortal man. She asked Zeus to make her lover both immortal and forever young. Zeus agreed reluctantly but also commanded Hypnos to induce eternal sleep in Selene's lover, which he did. Selene's lover never aged, never died, and never woke up. He was immortal and forever young.

The ancient story of sleep and aging also includes the god of medicine. Asklepios was said to be the son of Apollo and a mortal woman named Coronis. While Coronis was pregnant, she fell in love with a mortal man. When Apollo learned of the secret affair he killed Coronis and her lover. But, at the last moment, he took pity on his unborn child and cut the boy from his dying mother's womb. Apollo named the child Asklepios and he grew up to become the greatest physician who ever lived, the god of medicine.[47]

In time, Asklepios married Epione, the goddess of soothing comfort and the personification of the care needed for recovery. They had two daughters. Hygiea was associated with the prevention of illness and the continuation of good health. Her name is the source of the word "hygiene." Panacea embodied the idea that substances (we would call them medications) could cure sickness. Today we use the term "panacea" to refer to something that can quickly solve all problems.

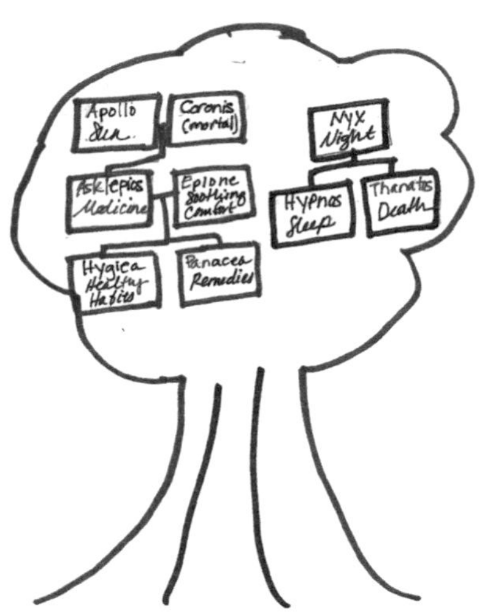

Ancient stories show us how people thought about sleep and healing long ago. For the Greeks, medicine (Asklepios) was not enough; they also needed soothing comfort (Epione). Sleep (Hypnos) was the brother of death (Thanatos) but also, and more hopefully, the father of dreams (Morpheus). We all need to sleep and to dream; indeed, we will die if those things are denied to us. But, sometimes, sleep eludes us.

Let's imagine a mortal woman, a loving wife, recently widowed. She yearns for the relief of sleep, but it does not come. Days, then weeks, pass. Hypnos is aware of her suffering but does not know how to help her. The widow's cries tug at his heart-strings and he resolves to visit the daughters of Asklepios (Hygiea and

Panacea) and ask for their assistance. He finds them in a forest glade and tells them of the widow's terrible insomnia...

Hygiea (the goddess of healthy habits): Does this person have healthy sleep habits?

Hypnos (the god of sleep): Habits? She doesn't need habits, she needs sleep! Can you help her?

Hygeia: I can help if you will answer my questions. The simple things, does she do the simple things well?

Hypnos: She lays down in her bed but cannot sleep. She is newly a widow. What else is there to say?

Hygiea: When her husband lived it was likely that they retired together for the evening. Now her bed is empty.

Does she still go to bed at the same time every night?

Hypnos: No, not often, why should that matter?

Hygeia: Going to bed and waking up at the same time every day instructs the body. It sets the rhythm by which we live.

Hypnos: When she does go to bed she tosses and turns, sometimes until the cock crows.

Hygiea: Mmmmhhh, this is a problem. She no longer associates her bed with restful sleep. Laying in bed awake for a long time can easily become a bad habit. When sleep does not come naturally it is better to get out of bed and do something else. It is especially good if these things are -- boring. She should have a basket of boring things that she can take up when sleep does not come.

Hypnos: Another thing, I've seen her put a kettle to boil and drink strong tea in the evening.

Panacea (Goddess of Remedies): Oh dear, that is not right. There are some teas that do help bring sleep and some that keep us awake. Do you know the name of the tea she drinks?

Hypnos: (Shrugs his shoulders and yawns) It is tea, that is all I know.

Panacea: It is better just to drink water before bedtime. She should save her tea leaves for the morning light.

Hypnos: (Nods in agreement) But the good news is that she sleeps most of the afternoon.

Hygiea: Napping?

Hypnos: (Smiling) Yes!

Hygiea: This is -- not so good. Naps should not be so long, it confuses the body. The mortals are creatures of habit yet they often forget that this is so. They teach their children well enough. There are bedtime stories and rituals for the little ones but when they mature they seem to forget the wisdom of the little things. Short naps are better than long naps.

Hypnos: It is well known that a warm bath can make children sleepy. The same is true for those who are old.

Panacea: Indeed, the bathwater warms the body and then, as it cools, drowsiness follows in its wake. It is natural for the body to cool in the evening.

The warm bath exaggerates the effect of helping bring sleep. Even soaking one's feet in warm water before bed can help bring on this effect.

Hypnos: In my palace in the realm of Hades it is always deliciously cool and dark. I sleep better there than anywhere else. I have a couch of ivory on which I can rest. So nice!

Panacea: (Looking at Hygiea) Yes, that really sounds -- delightful?

Hygiea: (Glaring at Panacea) I have heard that you keep gardens of poppies and herbs near your palace, ones that are known to induce sleep.

Panacea: Powerful potions have their place but must be used with caution; rarely should they be continued more than fourteen nights.

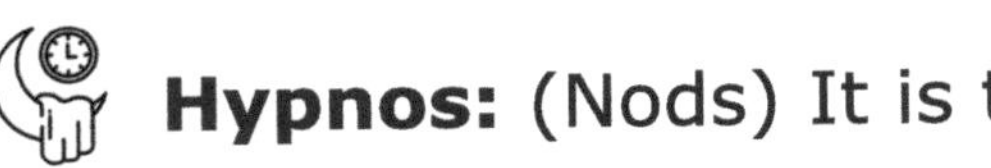

Hypnos: (Nods) It is true.

Hygiea: Now, about the widow, I suppose that her mind runs riot with memories, and fears, especially at night.

Hypnos: Indeed, the grief is greatest when she tries to rest.

Hygiea: When she struggles, I will whisper into the widow's ear: "Rise and take pen in hand. Write down all of your worries. Record all of your fears. When you are done, put the paper away. All your troubles will be waiting for you in the morning. Meanwhile, you may sleep and, perchance, dream of better things."

Morpheus (God of Dreams): (Rubbing the sleep from his eyes) Dreams? Did someone call my name?

Hypnos: (Smiling) The widow sleeps now. Go to her, my son, and grant her the sweetest dreams you have to offer.

Morpheus: (Smiling) It shall be as you wish, Father.

The struggle to understand simple things, like how to get a good night's sleep, has been going on for thousands of years. Science has added much to our understanding of human physiology, but has done little to improve on simple common sense.

Sleep Common Sense:

- **Beds are places for sleeping and should not become places of worry.**
- **Routines and rituals help sleep come to us more easily.**
- **Little things, like a warm bath, can help us fall asleep.**

Taken together, these simple practices are known as sleep hygiene (in honor of Hygeia). Improving our sleep hygiene costs nothing but can lead us toward better sleep and better sleep can lead us toward greater strength, purpose and belonging.

The Sixth Hour

"Happiness consists of getting enough sleep. Just that, nothing more."
— Robert A. Heinlein

There is a widespread, and nonsensical, notion that old people ought to sleep just like they did when they were young. Time changes our faces, our bones, our muscles and our minds. It also changes how we sleep. One reason people are not more aware of these changes is that, generally speaking, our sleep vocabulary is mostly limited to asking each other, "How did you sleep?" The answers we receive tend to run along the lines of "Great!" or "Terrible." We tend to expect that those who slept well will have an extra spring in their step and those who slept poorly to be more than a little grouchy.

Before we can master the secrets of sleep in the later decades of life we must get better at talking about sleep. We can start with these basic sleep-related terms:

- **Sleep Pressure:** Drowsiness that builds the longer we have been awake.
- **Sleep Opportunity:** The number of hours we set aside for sleep each day.
- **Sleep Latency:** The time it takes to fall asleep.
- **Sleep Deprivation**: Less than eight hours of sleep a night over a sustained period.
- **Sleep Rebound:** Recovering from sleep deprivation by experiencing an increased need for sleep for a period of time.
- **Sleep Inertia:** A period of sluggishness with decreased mental acuity and prolonged reaction times after deep sleep.

- **Phase Advance:** A shift in sleep cycle to rise earlier and retire earlier.
- **Monophasic Sleep:** One continuous sleep episode per day.
- **Biphasic Sleep:** Two sleep episodes per day, usually one long and one short.
- **Polyphasic Sleep**: Sleep episodes scattered across a 24 hour period.

Sleep Pressure:

Sleep pressure is experienced as a feeling of drowsiness that builds in intensity the longer we have been awake. Sometimes referred to as the "homeostatic sleep drive," sleep pressure is relieved by a restful period of sleep. We often experience increased sleep pressure when our immune system is fighting an infection.

Notably, this sleepiness is driven by compounds produced by

our immune system, not the virus or bacteria our body is fighting. Highly demanding mental or physical activities also increase sleep pressure. Experts advise that marathoners aim for 9 to 10 hours of sleep a night for the first few nights after a race.

Sleep Opportunity:

Our sleep opportunity consists of the number of hours we set aside for sleep each day. If we retire for the evening at 11:00 PM and rise at 6:00 AM we have created a seven hour sleep opportunity. This is not the same as the number of hours actually slept. Our total sleep per day can never exceed the sleep opportunity we make for ourselves.

Sleep Latency:

It is the amount of time it takes to fall asleep and can be shortened with bedtime rituals. Parents of young children are quite familiar with sleep latency. They carefully craft a bedtime routine for a toddler but instead of falling asleep their child issues a series of requests for water, a kiss, or one more bedtime story. When the parents finally go to bed they find that a worried mind can lead to tossing and turning -- and increase sleep latency.

Sleep Fragmentation:

Sleep fragmentation is characterized by repetitive short interruptions of sleep and tends to increase as we grow older.[48] The sleeper may not recall these episodes and might only be aware that something is wrong because they find themselves struggling against daytime drowsiness. Sleep fragmentation can be caused by a wide range of health and environmental factors.

Sleep Efficiency:

We can calculate our sleep efficiency by dividing the hours of sleep we get during a night by the number of hours of sleep opportunity we create for ourselves. Young people tend to have very high sleep efficiency and sleep efficiency has been shown to decrease with age.

Sleep Deprivation:

Most humans need about eight hours of sleep a night in order to remain healthy. People who get less than that amount of sleep over a sustained period are at risk for negative health consequences including hypertension, diabetes, obesity, depression, heart attack, and stroke. The medical literature makes it clear that sleep loss and sleep disorders have profound and widespread negative effects on human health.[49]

Sleep Rebound:

After a period of sleep deprivation all animals experience an increased need for sleep. College students often display sleep rebound when they return home after finals week. After the rebound period passes the animal (or college student) returns to a normal sleep pattern.

Sleep Inertia:

When we are woken from a deep sleep we often experience a period of sluggishness with decreased mental acuity and prolonged reaction times. People who feel "jet-lagged" often struggle with sleep inertia and find it difficult to "get going" in the morning when their sleep cycle is still set to a different time zone.

Phase Advance:

Many elders develop an advanced sleep phase syndrome that gradually changes the timing of sleep and the peak period of alertness. When this happens, people have difficulty staying awake unless they go to bed very early. They also wake up very early and find it hard to fall back to sleep. This condition is harmless except for the way it isolates people from the swirl of social life. On the upside, advanced sleep phase syndrome did give rise to the "early bird special" that offers low priced meals to people who want to eat dinner at four in the afternoon.

Monophasic Sleep:

When we experience sleep in one continuous episode per day our sleep can be said to be monophasic. Growing teenage boys are perhaps the best at this type of sleep.

Biphasic Sleep:

People who sleep twice a day (usually one long sleep episode at night and a short one during the day) are experiencing biphasic sleep. Young people and old people both show an affinity for biphasic sleep.

Polyphasic Sleep:

When our sleep periods are scattered across a 24 hour period we are experiencing polyphasic sleep. This is the sleep pattern newborns prefer. Polyphasic sleep can also re-emerge near the end of life.

What if there was a community of elders that responded to the modern epidemic of sleep deprivation by turning away from sleeping pills and looking instead toward ancient wisdom regarding sleep?

The Romans adopted a biphasic sleep pattern as their culture's norm. Here's how it worked. First, they divided the day into two parts. They called them ante-meridian (before noon) and post-meridian (after noon). We've kept this division although we refer to the parts of the day as "AM" and "PM." The first hour of the Roman day arrived with sunrise (not midnight as is customary for us) and work commenced as soon as there was light. By the sixth hour after sunrise, it was time for the midday meal -- and a nap.

The Latin words for the sixth hour are "sexta hora." The midday nap and meal were very popular, and many other cultures adopted these practic-es. In Spanish, "sexta hora" became "siesta."

In 21st century America, mono-phasic sleep is regarded as normal and everyone is encouraged to stay on a schedule that keeps them active during the day while sleeping at night. Parents, in particular, are eager to rush babies (who love poly-phasic sleep) into toddler-hood (where biphasic sleep is the rule) and on to childhood (and the embrace of monophasic sleep). But what about old age? Aging may provide us with an opportunity to shift away from the monophasic sleep we have been so long accustomed to, and embrace bi-phasic sleep. A midday meal followed by a short nap very likely suits older minds and bodies better than the practice of confining all sleep to the nighttime.

There is a general (if not openly stated) bias against naps and napping among adults. It is true that eccentric inventor types are lauded for their naps but regular folks are expected to power through the day no matter how drowsy they might feel. The Pew Research Center surveyed 1,488 adults on the subject of napping. They found that 41 percent of men over 50 reported taking a nap in the past day compared to just 28 percent of women who said the same. More than half of those over 80 reported taking a nap in the past 24 hours.

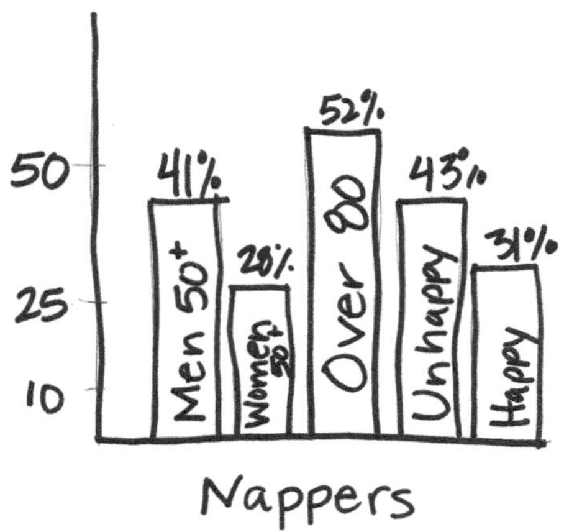

Interestingly, this research also suggests that nappers may be, slightly, less happy, and less healthy, than non-nappers.[50] The data shows that people who report feeling unhappy are more likely to report napping than people who say they are happy. Unhappy people are much also more likely to report having had trouble sleeping than people who say they are happy. This pattern also holds for health status. Unhealthy people report napping more often than healthy people and are more likely to report not sleeping well. Finally, old people who are having difficulty maintaining their independence reported having trouble sleeping and are more likely to take naps.

So what is going on here? Is napping a bad thing that only old, sick, unhappy people do? Not at all.

Because we live in a ramrodding, go go world, naps and napping have been relegated to the periphery of our society. As a result, daytime sleeping (napping) is employed by many people who are struggling to get all the sleep they need at night. They use naps as a way to address their problems with real sleep, and real sleep happens at night. This is not how the Romans saw things, or how siesta culture works today. The midday nap should be connected to the midday meal and, used correctly, can act to refresh and restore the napper in preparation for the second half of the day. This is biphasic sleep with honor, dignity, and purpose.

Done right, the midday nap can reduce fatigue, elevate mood, boost memory, and stimulate alertness.

The secret to success lies in developing good nap hygiene:

- **Duration: 15-30 minutes.**
- **Timing: Earlier in the day, around 6 hours after waking.**
- **Location: A quiet, comfortable place in a restful position.**

A nap should last about 15 to 30 minutes (one study suggested that the perfect nap duration is 28 minutes). Longer naps increase the risk of an unpleasant encounter with sleep inertia. Waking up from a nap feeling groggy and tired wipes out the nap's potential benefits and can increase the risk of poor sleep the following night.[51]

Timing is also important. Romans napped at the "sixth hour" of their day perhaps because they knew that napping later in the afternoon could make it harder to fall asleep at night. If possible, naps should be taken while in a restful position and in a quiet, comfortable environment. At the nap's end, it is best to return to wakefulness slowly and gently.

Developing a deeper understanding of sleep and its power to heal makes Stella's story even more painful to read. Her stroke was a serious matter but the institutions she was admitted to and transferred to made the job of recovery vastly more difficult because they paid no heed to her pressing need for sleep.

Everything would have gone differently for her if a "Sleep Coach" had been given the opportunity to craft means and circumstances that would ensure Stella slept well and fully each and every day of her recovery and rehabilitation.

Heal

Not all myths are ancient, or even old. Modern myths tell us what we are supposed to believe about the world we live in, and how it works. One of the most powerful of the modern myths centers on doctors, nurses, and hospitals. Generations of Americans were reared on stories of dashing doctors and compassionate nurses battling death and disease. Among the most famous of the televised medical dramas is *General Hospital* which premiered on April 1, 1963 and was still on the air nearly 60 years later.

Because they were fictional doctors and nurses, and because the writers had to hold the audience's interest, the diagnosis and treatment of illness (and sometimes injuries) followed a well-worn narrative arc.

In real life, however, medical care is messy, frustrating and, too often, disappointing. On television, unusual medical conditions are diagnosed swiftly and accurately. In real life, an accurate diagnosis can be preceded by years of testing, false hopes, consultations and telling one's story over and over again, hoping to be believed. Television doctors always know the right things to say and do. Real world doctors often fumble for the right words, suggest medications that don't work, and become frustrated with patients who fail to respond to the prescribed treatment.

While it is true that we now possess treatments so powerful and effective that our ancestors could scarcely have dreamed of them, modern medicine also does a great deal of harm. Nearly every family has a story to tell about an older relative whose life came to ruin because of medical complications and complications resulting from the treatment of those complications. Far too often, the health care system violates medicine's golden rule, "First, do no harm."

Slow Medicine

At the time of America's founding, medicine was a minor profession with limited practical and economic significance. Dr. Benjamin Rush, a signer of the Declaration of Independence, considered the lancet (a special knife used to drain blood from patients' veins) his most important medical instrument. Much less admirably, he adamantly refused to reconsider dangers that "bleeding" posed to patients even as the practice fell out of favor.

Dr. Rush would be amazed by the sprawling and tremendously complex system of hospitals, clinics, professions, government programs, and insurance companies that we see today. He might also point out that the damage done by his lancet was minor compared to the adverse events, complications, and side-effects that run rampant in that system. Millions of old people and their families have been promised a carefully coordinated continuum of care. What they actually get is a one-way ride on a "sick care roller coaster."

The power to heal includes the power to harm. Far too often, the power to harm exceeds our health care system's power to heal.

This story begins on a cold, rainy Friday afternoon. The date was December 13, 1799. George Washington's grandson later recalled, "The improver remained so long exposed to the inclemency of the weather as to be considerably wetted before his return to the house."[52] After a quiet evening of work in his study, the master of the house retired to his bed but found "feverish restlessness and pain" in the place of rest and comfort.

The next morning brought weather that was colder still. The plantation's overseer was called to the house and he removed a pint of blood from Washington. By midday a physician was summoned. A blister was applied to the throat and another pint of blood was let. At three o'clock in the afternoon, two other doctors came to consult with the first, and, by a vote of two to one, they decided to let more blood, removing another two pints. They reported that the blood flowed "slow and thick." Washington grew weaker still. In a hoarse whisper he told his oldest friend, "I am dying, sir—but am not afraid to die."

The end, his grandson lamented, came swiftly: "Composing his form at length, and folding his arms on his bosom, without a sigh, without a groan, the Father of his Country died." In their struggle to heal, George Washington's doctors violated medicine's most important law.

Nearly two centuries later two of geriatric medicine's wisest elders (Drs. Knight Steel and T. Franklin Williams) published an article titled "It's Time to March."[53] In it, they argued that a specialist-dominated, technology-oriented health care industry was addicted to the practice of "fast medicine" and was failing to meet its stated goal of healing the sick and injured. They were especially concerned about the damage fast medicine was doing to old people.

Dennis McCullough accepted the challenge issued by Drs. Steel and Williams. His book, My Mother, Your Mother: Embracing "Slow Medicine," outlines a radically different approach to health and well-being.54 McCullough cites research that suggests combining a teamwork-oriented approach with effective, unhurried communication. He argues that helping health-care providers, families, friends, neighbors, and elders to work together is vital to success. Slow Medicine also emphasizes the value of sometimes difficult and long-avoided conversations. Learning how people really feel about issues related to comfort, honor, dignity and the end of life can do much to minimize inappropriate, often dangerous medical interventions.

While fast medicine's awe-inspiring technology continues to dominate the world of health care, the inspiration behind "slow medicine" has the potential to change how medicine is practiced. Thoughtful conversations, skillful teamwork, and a deep respect for the individual don't come naturally to those schooled in the ways of fast medicine but they have proven their worth for those willing to try them. Slowing down and getting clear can help everyone involved find right answers that are hidden from those who go too fast.

Consider, for example, the quickest, easiest response any fast medicine doctor has to any complicated problem. She can reach for a prescription pad and say, "Let's try this, I think it might help." When this happens repeatedly an old person's list of medications grows. When this happens on a society-wide scale, we wind up with an epidemic of poly-pharmacy, taking more than five prescriptions daily. In fact, the overuse and misuse of medications has become a major source of sickness and death among old people. A 2008 study demonstrated that nearly 30 percent of people over the age of 65 were taking six or more different medications and more than 15 percent had been prescribed one or more potentially inappropriate medications, and those numbers have continued to climb. We hope that medicines will make us better but as the number of daily prescribed medications grows so does a person's risk of hospitalization, and death.[55]

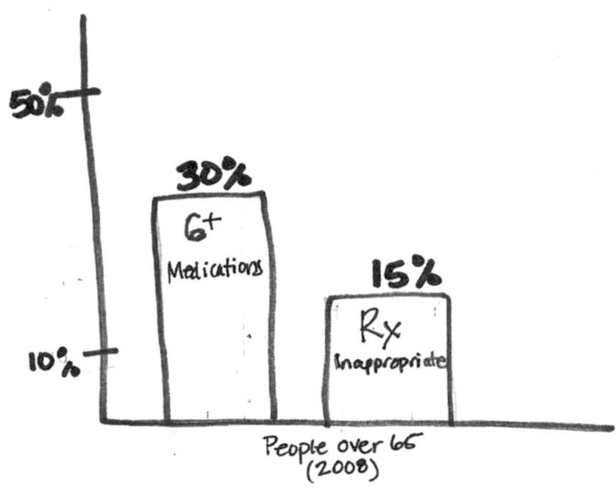

Mary Knudsen peered over the top of her glasses and repeated the words "brown bag drug evaluation" in a tone of voice that made it clear that she thought her niece was being ridiculous. "I heard what you said but I still don't see why I should go through the bother, I only take what my doctors tell me to." Her eyes narrowed. "You think I'm a drug addict or something?"

"No, I don't," her niece answered, "but look at all these bottles. It's like you're running a pill factory or something." She gestured at a dining room table littered with amber plastic containers. "And we haven't even started on the supplements."

"Bah!"

Two hours later, a double-bagged collection of medications, creams, vitamins, minerals and berry extracts sat on the exam room table and Dr. Ansel Morris was eager to dig in.

"Let's see what we've got here."

"It's what my doctors ordered," Mary insisted.

"I have no doubt that you are right," Dr. Morris agreed.

He plunged his hand into the sack and drew out a bottle of Darvon.

"I think those are my pain pills."

"Pain?" he asked.

"For when I hurt my back."

"It says here that they were prescribed in 1997."

"Waste not, want not," Mary said.

Dr. Morris opened the container and looked inside. "They're covered in mold." He turned the bottle upside down. "And stuck to the bottom. We'll dispose of them for you."

Mary nodded.

He fished for another bottle. "Digoxin? I didn't know you took this."

"My heart doctor gave it to me."

"Do you take it?"

"Once in a while. I take one whenever I feel my heart skip a beat."

"Good news!" Dr. Morris said. "You don't need it anymore. We can get rid of it."

"If you're sure."

"Yes, I am sure."

And so it went, with the Benadryl, Pamelor, Ativan, Meclizine, Seroquel, niacin, Norpace, Tigan, Ditropan and cyclobenzaprine.

Ansel Morris rubbed his eyes. "Halfway there."

Mary grunted, "The rest is vitamins and I suppose you'll tell me I don't need vitamins."

"It's better to get your vitamins from good food than from a bottle," Dr. Morris said. "People waste boatloads of money buying supplements they don't really need."

"Not me."

"We'll see."

Dr. Morris lined up a row of vitamin bottles. "You're taking way too much niacin, thiamine and B12. Too much vitamin C, too much magnesium and way too much selenium."

"Yeah, too much of everything."

"Nope," Dr. Morris replied, "you are not getting enough vitamin D or calcium."

"Good for the bones."

"They sure are."

"You don't need the vitamin E either; it is probably interfering with your blood thinner."

Dr. Morris found the bottom of the brown bag. "Almost done. Fish Oil?"

"Dr. Oz says it will keep me young."

"Is it working?"

Mary grinned. "No."

"Didn't think so. Don't need it."

Dr. Morris worked his way through the bottles of shark cartilage, St. John's wort, feverfew, ma huang and ginkgo. "Not my ginkgo, I need my ginkgo."

"What for?"

"Dr. Oz says I'll lose my mind if I don't take my ginkgo!"

"No you won't. There is nothing wrong with your mind and you know it."

"Of course there isn't," Mary smirked.

"Studies show that ginkgo doesn't prevent dementia."

Again, she peered imposingly over the tops of her glasses. "You're sure?"

"I'm sure," he answered.

"OK."

Mary's niece finally spoke up. "So this is it? Just three medications, Vitamin D and a calcium pill?"

Dr. Morris eyed the list he'd made. "Yep, that's it."

"I've got," Mary said, "I don't know, maybe 10 doctors, hard to keep them straight. They gonna be mad that you're bossing them around?"

Dr. Morris crossed his arms and leaned back against the exam room wall. "Actually, they'll be glad to hear that we took the time to straighten this all out."

Mary hesitated, "I leave it all here, just take these home with me?"

"Yep."

"You'll tell all those other fellows about this?"

"Sure will."

Mary smiled, "Doc, I gotta say, my sciatica is acting up again and I wanna know what you're gonna do about it..."

People make fun of Goldilocks but the girl had a point. It isn't too hard or too soft, too hot or too cold, or too much or too little that matters -- what matters is getting things just right. Taking the maximum number of medications might kill you. Taking the minimum number of medications might leave you with untreated pain or a smoldering infection.

Taking the optimum number of medications, (the right meds at the right dose, at the right time, for the right reason) offers the best path to better health and wellness.

"Fast medicine" favors more treatment over optimum treatment. Dr. Goldilocks practices slow medicine. She's always trying to get things "just right."

Gero-Transcendance

Lars Tornstam wrote the first Swedish thesis in the field of gerontological sociology in 1973. He went on to build an international reputation, publishing dozens of research papers and leading the Social Gerontology Group. He is best known, though, as the creator of the theory of Gero-transcendence. His model broke from the orthodox view that aging was exclusively a process of decline. Instead, he argued, aging is a key that unlocks a trove of rich developmental potential. In particular, he found that old people often engineer a decisive shift away from the materialistic and mechanistic point of view that dominates the middle phase of the life cycle.

Typical of his work is a paper that presents in-depth interviews with Swedish men and women aged

52 to 97 years. He found patterns in the self-reported changes that his interviewees were experiencing. As Tornstam began to better understand these changes, he sorted them into three categories.[56]

1. Self
2. Relationships
3. The Cosmos

Tornstam's showed that many normal, healthy old people engage in a sustained re-evaluation of the self. This process often reveals previously hidden aspects of the self, both good and bad. It is also associated with a growing awareness that "I" and "me" are not the actual center of the universe. The softening of adulthood's ego-centricity accompanies a shift away from egoism and toward altruism. Young people have long observed that old people take pleasure in recounting episodes from early in their lives. Tornstam argues that reminiscence of this type is connected to a deeply considered revision of an elder's life story.

The character and importance of social connections also change in late life. Overall, old people tend to become more selective with regard to who they want to spend time with; generally speaking, they value solitude more, and superficial relationships less. The connection to established social roles and rules also loosens. This can manifest in a newfound pleasure in transcending social norms. "When I get old I will wear purple."

Many people find that they become increasingly aware of the large gray areas that emerge between right and wrong, and are less eager to tell others how they should behave.

Most of the people who are growing old in the 21st Century were taught that time and space are strictly fixed, unchanging entities. Aging can, however, lead people to challenge this certainty. Past and present become less distinct and some people report feeling the immediate presence of long-absent relatives. These changes may lead to an interest in genealogy, and one's relationship with past generations. This "cosmic" perspective also seems to be associated with a receding fear of death and growing curiosity about "What comes next?"

Obviously, not all of the people studied by Tornstam have shared all of these experiences. The theory of gero-transcendence suggests a general pattern of development that can unfold in the late decades of life. It acknowledges the reality of decline in physical and mental processes but places those changes into a broader, more meaningful context. Tornstam found that those who did experience changes of this type were generally happier and more satisfied with life than those who did not.

While it is easy to propose and test theories of child (and even adult) development, Tornstam's task was much more difficult. Young people, especially the youngest, are quite similar to one another. Old people of the same age show much more diversity, making it much harder to craft general statements about them. Far from being a weakness or defect, this variability is among the greatest gifts that longevity offers us.

The reinterpretation of self, society, and even the cosmos, is work that requires a lifetime of preparation. The existence of a drive to transcend ordinary understandings of life and living is, if Tornstam is to be believed, an important and distinctively human attribute. This perspective provides a useful way of viewing the difficulties that younger people face when they seek transcendent experiences in their own lives. Recent developments in neurobiology connect the experiences of transcendentalists, young and old, with specific processes related to healthy aging.

The millennia-old practice of meditation and the quieting of the mind have, in recent years, been studied carefully by Western medical science. Brain scans performed during meditation have demonstrated that the experience of transcendence is associated with (among other things) a decrease in activity in the prefrontal cortex. Some have called this part of the brain "the monkey mind." It seems to be the seat of the familiar strivings, anxieties, and obsessions that we associate with the ego and its needs.

Surprisingly, research conducted on old people has also shown a decline in the activity of the prefrontal cortex and the neurons that connect it to the rest of the brain.[57] This is interesting because people often think of meditation as a good thing and aging as a bad thing.

The shift in brain activity away from the prefrontal cortex and a decrease in dopaminergic neurotransmitter activity would, ordinarily, be used as evidence to support the declinist view of age and aging.

It is true, after all, that the human brain shrinks with age and the prefrontal cortex shrinks faster than the rest of the brain. These changes are objective, measurable, and have been verified by numerous investigators. The declinist view of aging interprets these changes solely as a catalogue of losses. Declinism also blinds us to the new capabilities that these changes may be instrumental in unleashing.

Actively searching for the hidden powers of age, as Tornstam has done, lets us ask and then attempt to answer the question, "Does normal aging open a shortcut to transcendental experiences?" Our brains change in countless ways as we age; perhaps some of those changes carry the currently unappreciated benefit of loosening the grip that the ego has upon the self. This, as many world religions attest, may be the greatest of all possible human victories.

There is great power hidden within old age, but we will remain ignorant of the depth and breadth of that power as long as we insist on measuring elders using metrics better suited to young people. A more useful approach would be to chart—in the context of old age itself—the changes in human capacity that aging calls forth.

We see what we look for and we look for what we know.

We "know" that youth represents a special sort of perfection. This assumption is, however, really nothing more than ageist prejudice. Worse, it also leads us away from what might best be called the treasures of aging.

Growing old is a difficult project. The mismeasure of aging makes it more difficult still. Ageist prejudice insists on imagining a monstrous old age that bristles with disease, disability, dependence, decline, and ultimately, death. It is no wonder so many of us deny our own aging and search for anti-aging miracles that might save us. Recasting aging as a search for buried treasure that is free for the taking offers us a new pathway to healing.

Life gets better when we transcend our fears, cease fretting about what has been lost, and set out in search of riches yet to be discovered.

Finding New Normals

Healing, true healing, is not what we suppose it to be. A half century of popular medical dramas have given us the idea that to be healed (in the span of a single episode no less) is to return to the way things used to be. Healing of this sort exists mainly in the realm of fiction because the real world simply does not work this way. When we lose a spouse, or a lung, or a child, or a breast -- we can never go back. We can never return to life as it used to be. It is human nature, however, to wish that we could, and to yearn for what has been lost. The trouble comes when we can not let go of what was and begin to explore what might be.

Healing is not a return to the way things were, it is moving forward to find a new normal.

In every grief there must be a turning. We must eventually shift our focus away from our loss and begin to look toward our future. Many people resist this turning thinking that, somehow, moving forward dishonors the memory of those we've loved and lost. After the death of Prince Albert in 1861, Queen Victoria wore widow's weeds (dark, somber outfits intended to show respect for the deceased) until her death. To lose Albert, she said, was "like tearing the flesh from my bones."[58] But her flesh and bones endured another 40 years.

Victoria grieved for decades but failed to grasp the purpose of grief. Grief fills the terrible void between what was and what will be. Gradually, it grants us permission to think of the future again and thus begin the struggle to find our new normal. This is difficult work and modern "fast" medicine has almost nothing helpful to say on the subject. We are better off studying the example set by those who have lost, grieved, and begun again. Amputees have much to teach us about this process. They knew who they were when they had four limbs. But they must all face the question, "Who am I now?" What part of me was lost and what part remains? What place does this new me have in the world? Am I ready to begin again?

True healing occurs when we are delivered from one way of living, and into another.

Each new normal is different from the last and may yield greater happiness, or less. No one can say for sure. It is estimated that in all of human history about 17 billion people have walked the earth. Out of that 17 billion, not one ever grew a new limb. Not one ever grew young again. The truth of human experience provides all the proof we need -- we can never go back, we can only move forward.

Like Victoria, some people resist the call of a new life, a new normal. That is their right. But looking backward does isolate us from the world as it is. Grief is a lonely affair that can too easily separate us from the people who love us and want us to be well. It can also rob us of the feeling of being at home, of living a life of meaning and purpose. Unable to release our claim on the life we still feel should be ours, we are undone.

Helping people in this situation is a delicate art. Some favor the "Listen here! It's time for you to stop with this nonsense, pull yourself up by your bootstraps, and get on with it!" school of counseling. It isn't as if this never works. But, really, it almost never works. After all, these admonitions reveal much more about the speaker's own fears and anxieties. Others attempt to bring reason and common sense to bear: "Surely it is not practical to carry on this way." Well, no, it is not practical but practicality has nothing to do with our struggle to contend with loss. Victoria was not being practical, she was doing the best she could. Our best is all any of us can do, and there is no shame in that.

We have rituals and ceremonies that help us say goodbye to departed loved ones. We also need rituals and ceremonies that help us say goodbye to old normals. After all, the way we lived before remains dear to us, even after it is gone. Properly grieving the loss of an old normal puts us on the path to finding a new normal. It opens the way to a growing understanding that this is "how I live now."

New normals contain things we like, things we detest, things we love, and things we discover. They also hold the memories of what we have lost. As our new normal becomes "how I live now" our old normal fades into "how I lived then." This is why people so often reckon time in terms of normals. When someone says, "It's been three years since the accident," we know precisely what they mean. One normal was wrenched from their grasp, and another has taken its place. Among the living, it is old people who have the greatest experience, knowledge and facility with finding new normals. After all, they have been practicing this art for 80, 90, or even 100 years.

A fifteenth century folk saying grasps a truth that too often eludes modern medicine.

"To cure sometimes, to relieve often, and to comfort always."[59]

This aphorism is often thought to refer to physicians, and doctors would be wise to heed its counsel. But it actually addresses us all. We all seek new normals, we all seek healing. We are all healers.

We must know that no matter how big the hospital might be, or how advanced its technology might become, the cures we seek will only come to us -- sometimes. Misery, grief and pain abound and, more often than we suppose, we can relieve others of burdens they do not need to carry. Then we can do the same for ourselves. The admonition to provide comfort is often interpreted as a summons to care for those who are dying but it applies with even greater force to the living. Life is difficult and it is the care and kindness we give, and receive, that eases our singular passage from birth to death.

To heal is to comfort -- always.

Afterword

In 1989, a nurse named Connie Evashwick published an article that set off a revolution in health care. In it, she coined the term "continuum of care" which she defined as an "integrated system of care that guides and tracks patients over time through a comprehensive array of health services spanning all levels of intensity of care."[60]

For the next three decades virtually every health care executive with system-level responsibilities worked hard to develop and refine a continuum of care. Rarely, if ever, did they stop to ask if this was the right thing to do.

The "continuum of care" concept eventually transformed health care in ways that were

pleasing to executives, and daunting for old people and their families.

While their board presentations showed patients flowing smoothly from the Emergency Department to the ICU to Med/Surg to Inpatient Rehab to Long-Term Care, that is not what people actually experienced. True, they were admitted, transferred and released from various "levels of care," but people contended with a reality that was, and remains, hidden from the professionals. They confronted the terrifying gaps that divide the so-called continuum.

An Emergency Department physician can diagnose, treat and admit a patient and feel, rightfully, that his or her work is well done. The patient and the family, however, experience a five-hour wait for a "bed" to be made ready followed by a bumptious admission process that requires them to repeat almost everything they have already said about the history of the present illness, medications and co-morbidities. Nothing about this process feels "continuous" to them. People encounter acute illnesses and injuries as fearful episodes that threaten to turn their lives upside down. Professionals, in contrast, concentrate on the consistency and quality of "their" segment of care. Ordinarily, clinicians show little interest in what happens to patients when they enter the gaps between care segments.

The pursuit of a continuum of care rewards clinicians and administrators for focusing intensely on the metrics that apply to each level of care. This can work to people's advantage; for example, when a Joint Replacement Center performs a single task exceptionally well. Because they are only paid for services delivered in their segment, however, specialists spend little time considering what happens outside of their specific area of responsibility.

Indeed, organizational charts used by health care systems mostly show segments connected directly to each. They omit the gaps because the organization's leaders don't experience the gaps. A simple diagram, drawn from the administration's point of view, might divide the continuum of care into four segments. In the diagram below, A represents the most acute segment (perhaps post-operative cardiac patients) and D represents the least acute setting (perhaps a long-term care facility).

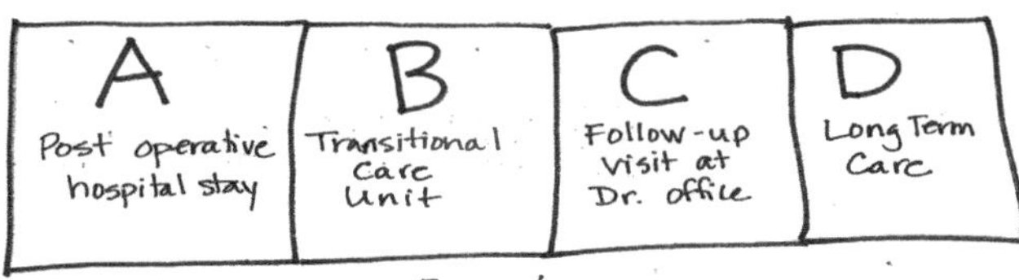

Figure 1

It would be terrific if elders did experience health care as a seamless journey that flowed effortlessly from one segment to the next, but they don't. In fact, old people and their families often find the gaps between segments of care to be the most distressing part of a clinical episode. People wonder why they have to repeat basic information so many times to so many people. Why basic information does not get transferred. Why tests and procedures have to be duplicated. The reality is that information leaks into the gaps between segments of care and is lost. When that happens, it is the patient who pays the price.

When confronted by an illness or injury there is nothing about the experience that suggests the existence of a seamless "continuum of care." Instead people pass through what might better be called a "continuum of experience."

Drawn as a diagram this continuum of experience would reveal the gaps that are a significant part of that experience.

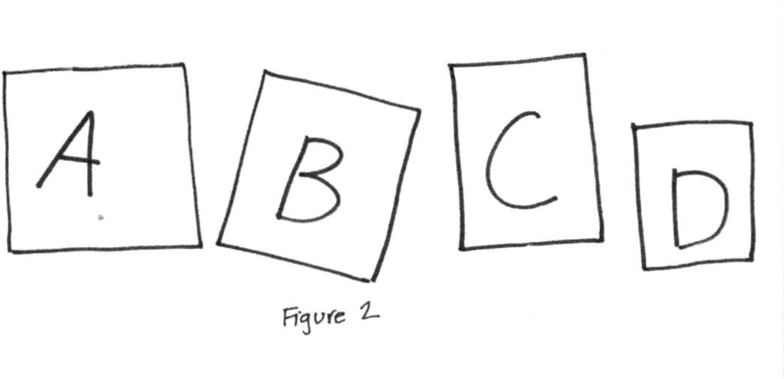

Figure 2

While these gaps are nearly invisible to clinicians and administrators, they exact a toll from the patients and families who must traverse them. The investment of time and energy in the work of "transition" and "navigation" is considerable, especially for elders. These costs ought to be included in our accounting of the total health care budget but are not. Instead, they function as a hidden tax on the finances, resources, and energy of elders and their families.

Few health care professionals ever "mind the gaps" because specialization offers a much faster path to success. Specialization flourishes because it allows professionals and administrators to focus on tightly defined tasks and procedures. Unfortunately, this inward focus also fuels a trend toward greater specialization and further divides the continuum of experience. Instead of the four segment continuum shown in Figure 1, people must contend with something more like an eight segment continuum.

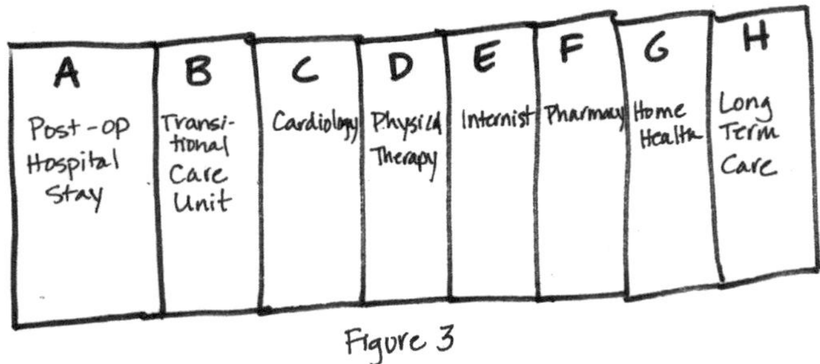

Figure 3

When we add the gaps that complete the "continuum of experience" we get Figure 4.

Figure 4

Comparing Figure 2 to Figure 4 reveals that doubling the number of clinical segments in the continuum also doubles the number of gaps between the segments. A person moving across the continuum of experience shown in Figure 2 must contend with three gaps between its segments. A patient with an identical clinical course in a more specialized system (Figure 4) must navigate the seven gaps between its segments. Elders and their families are compelled to invest time and effort in the work of traversing each of these gaps and must do so even when their resources are limited.

Figure 4 also highlights the fact that during a single clinical episode a patient confronted by a highly specialized continuum will spend less time in each segment. For example, in Figure 1 a patient's time in segment A would account for about 25% of the total episode of care. In the more specialized continuum sketched in Figure 3, segment A occupies only about 12% of the total episode of care. In the first example, a gap exists between units that have tended to the patient for a relatively large portion of the clinical episode. Because they are less specialized, it is also easier for them to maintain a more general awareness of the person as an individual. Greater specialization comes at a cost of weakened relationships and more fleeting personal interactions.

The continuing division of health care labor has done much to improve the technical proficiency of professionals and has spawned a crop of new specialties. It is not just "doctors and nurses" anymore. Nowadays we are tended by rehabilitation specialists, geriatric case managers, pharmacy consultants, and, increasingly, navigation coaches. All of these professionals need to be included in the process of transferring patients from one setting to another. The greater the number of disciplines involved, the more likely it becomes that errors will creep into the clinical experience and that valuable information will become "lost in the gaps." Despite these shortcomings, standardization and specialization continue to serve as the foundations for almost all health care services planning. We may, however, be approaching the point of diminishing returns and it is entirely possible to take specialization too far.

In 1985, The New York Times reported on the work of Svyatoslav N. Fyodorov and his "Medical Factory No. 1." At its peak, more than a thousand patients passed through Fyodorov's microsurgical assembly line every day. "The patients glide past in a steady stream, their vital signs and computerized diagnoses clipped to their cots. Lying on tables that are mounted on polished rails, they arrive through a port in the wall. Five doctors in surgical masks and gowns sit arrayed over matching microscopes in a room of gleaming stainless steel. As if on cue, they bend over five patients. About two minutes later they lean back, and the operating tables shift one position over for the next stage of the operation."

Dr. Fyodorov might have gotten a bit carried away with the division of labor. It is also true that many American professionals are also conveniently blind to the problems created by over-standardization in our own system. Elders, in particular, would benefit from a movement toward "de-specialization." The creation of a continuum of experience with fewer segments would help professionals get to know and focus more effectively on the people they are tending to. Unfortunately, "de-specialization" continues to be a fringe concept, as yet unloved and unexplored.

Most of the energy related to health care reform has actually been invested in an effort to help patients and their families navigate growing complexity and spawned by the subdivision of health care labor. The Coleman Care Transitions Intervention, developed by Eric Coleman, M.D., M.P.H., and the Naylor Transitional Care Model, developed by Mary Naylor, Ph.D., R.N., both aim to equip patients with the knowledge and tools they need to "take a more active role in their health care." The Coleman model, in particular, uses transition coaches to offer patients:

- Skills related to the self-management of medications.
- Support for maintaining a personal health record.
- Encouragement to schedule appointment(s) with the primary care provider or specialist as soon as possible after discharge.
- Education about health status "red flags" that indicate that one's condition is changing for the worse.

While Coleman and Naylor's work has proven its worth by reducing hospital readmissions, these initiatives do not address the larger challenge being faced by elders and their families. Nearly all patient navigation initiatives concentrate their efforts on managing the transition from the hospital to a "post-hospital" setting; this might be a private home, rehabilitation unit or nursing home. These "navigation" models fail to acknowledge the continuum of experience.

People living through acute clinical episodes know all too well that the shift from hospital to post-hospital is just one of a large number of transitions that are scattered before them like land mines. Coleman and Naylor simply accept the current highly segmented health care delivery system as a given and, in doing so, restrict the scope and potential impact of their own work. Offering improved navigation services inside a complex and confusing system is a good thing but "doing navigation better" is simply not enough. As Drs. Steel and Williams said, "It's time to march."

LEADS

Elders learn how to live abundant lives with "energy budgets" that have fewer reserves than those of young people. (More on this in *Aging Magnificently*, another book in this series). Given this, it would make sense to create an alternative delivery system that conserves, rather than squanders, that energy. Florence Nightingale had much to say about the importance of taking the patient's perspective fully into account. She observed that, "Apprehension, uncertainty, waiting, expectation, fear of surprise, do a patient more harm than any exertion. Remember he is face to face with his enemy all the time." It is unwise to tax the reserves of any patient but doing so is doubly foolish when age has already diminished a person's reserves of energy.

Every ounce of energy that older patients divert toward the complexities of navigating a highly segmented continuum of experience is an ounce of energy not expended on healing. Now, there is a better way. LEADS was created by Lifespark founder Joel Theisen. Trained as a nurse, he is unsparing in his critique of the "roller coaster" clinical course that too often defines the lives of elders and offers a vision of health and well-being defined by people not imposed by institutions.

LEADS stands for:
Life
Experience
Alternative
Delivery
System

Each of these terms deserves a bit of exploration. We use the term "life experience" to describe living the life we want, the life we choose for ourselves. This is what matters most to people. It is possible, for example, to be completely healthy, from a medical point of view, and also completely miserable. LEADS helps people break free from the sick care system and offers them new ways of gaining access to the services and supports that can help them live life as they choose.

LEADS also shifts the focus away from facilities and institutions and toward homes and communities. LEADS is driven by the idea that, while medical treatment is necessary (and often very effective), it's best used to battle disease -- not as the basis of a life worth living. The LEADS model embraces all of medicine's most powerful technologies but puts them into the context of what people want, what matters most to them. It uses a six step process to help people build a life plan with life changing power.

Discover -- Thoughtful conversations help us identify what matters most to us.

Prioritize -- It is easy to get sidetracked, confused and discouraged if we don't take time to slow down and get clear.

Empower -- Breaking out of an established routine and doing something new takes real effort and it is important to not waste time and energy along the way. There is no substitute for having access to the knowledge and tools that can speed us on our way.

Ignite -- When we challenge ourselves to embrace a goal something changes inside of us. Verbalizing a goal puts us "on the record" with the universe.

Measure -- Those who seek growth and improvement over time need to track their progress along the way.

Life Plans are populated by jointly developed, specific, measurable goals that map a pathway to greater health and well-being. Just as medical treatment plans are constantly revised and improved, a Life Plan is a living document that evolves over time. Wellness is no accident; it takes thought, partnership, persistence, and tangible measurements to bring it forth. The current healthcare system is designed to deliver ever more treatment and clinical services. LEADS is engineered to bring forth the strength, purpose and belonging we need to live life on our own terms. (Detailed examples of LEADS are featured in *The Good Life*, another book in this series).

Endnotes

1 N Engl J Med. 2013 Jan 10; 368(2): 100–102.

2 https://leaps.org/anti-aging-pioneer-aubrey-de-grey-people-middle-age-now-fair-chance/particle-13

3 https://www.cleveland.com/medical/2008/05/does_roizens_vision_of_longevi.html

4 Herodotus, Book III: 23

5 https://www.folklore.ee/folklore/vol16/tbilisi.pdf

6 https://whyy.org/articles/at-the-fountain-of-youth-irony-is-an-age-defying-mineral/

7 https://www.marketwatch.com/story/10-things-the-anti-aging-industry-wont-tell-you-2014-02-11

8 https://www.bustle.com/articles/136863

9 Butler, Kurt; Rayner, Lynn. (1985). The Best Medicine: The Complete Health and Preventive Medicine Handbook. Harper & Row, Publishers, San Francisco. pp. 133-135.

10 Cramp, Arthur J. (1936). Nostrums and Quackery and Pseudo-Medicine, Volume 3. Press of American Medical Association. pp. 145-147

11 The Fountain of Age Betty Friedan Simon and Schuster

12 https://plantsinmotion.bio.indiana.edu/

13 https://www.nps.gov/articles/worldmigration.htm

14 https://www.smithsonianmag.com/smart-news/bird-designed-jet-fighter-sets-new-record-longest-non-stop-bird-migration

15 https://mspmag.com/arts-and-culture/the-man-who-walked-around-the-world

16 https://www.npr.org/2015/05/31/410855681

17 https://pmj.bmj.com/content/90/1059/26

18 Upright and uptight: the invention of posture | by Tom Jesson.

19 https://medium.com/@thomas_jesson/upright-and-uptight-the-invention-of-posture-fe48282a4487

20 Stand Up Straight!: A History of Posture By Sander L. Gilman

21 https://link.springer.com/article/10.1007/s10912-013-9266-0

22 The Rise and Fall of American Posture David Yosifon and Peter N. Stearns The American Historical Review Vol. 103, No. 4 (Oct., 1998), pp. 1057-1095 (39 pages)

23 https://www.nhs.uk/conditions/kyphosis/treatment/

24 There are types of kyphosis that are caused by injuries and deformities of the spine. They are not considered here.

25 https://pubmed.ncbi.nlm.nih.gov/31322562/

26 Occup. Med. Vol. 47.112-116, 1997

27 Loudon, Swift & Bell 2008

28 https://logosatwork.com/ah-memories-presidential-fitness-challenge/

29 https://www.sbnation.com/2015/7/31/9038201/the-sad-sad-stories-of-the-presidential-fitness-test

30 https://www.ncoa.org/healthy-aging/falls-prevention/

31 http://www.cdc.gov/homeandrecreationalsafety/falls/adultfalls.html

32 https://www.ncbi.nlm.nih.gov/pmc/articles/PMC2849909/
33 https://www.ncbi.nlm.nih.gov/pmc/articles/PMC4589891/#R26
34 https://www.ellynsatterinstitute.org/family-meals-focus/79-you-dont-have-to-starve-children-to-make-them-eat/
35 Mattes RD, Hollis J, Hayes D, Stunkard AJ J Am Diet Assoc. 2005 May; 105(5 Suppl 1):S87-97.

36 https://www.ncbi.nlm.nih.gov/pmc/articles/PMC4772033/
37 Effects of anorexia on mortality among older adults receiving home care: an observation study. *Landi F, Liperoti R, Lattanzio F, Russo A, Tosato M, Barillaro C, Bernabei R, Onder G J Nutr Health Aging. 2012 Jan; 16(1):79-83.*

38 https://www.healthline.com/health/living-without-your-sense-of-smell
39 https://aginginplace.org/the-facts-behind-senior-hunger/
40 https://www.medicareadvantage.com/senior-hunger-in-america
41 https://www.cdc.gov/pcd/issues/2018/18_0058.htm
42 https://www.webmd.com/food-recipes/news/20090323/7-rules-for-eating
43 https://www.webmd.com/sleep-disorders/sleep-habits-assessment
44 N Engl J Med. 2013 Jan 10; 368(2): 100–102.
45 http://www.quotationspage.com/quote/1735.html

46 Macbeth William Shakespeare

47 Asklepios means "to cut open" and likely refers to the circumstances of the god's birth.

48 https://erj.ersjournals.com/content/17/4/723

49 https://www.ncbi.nlm.nih.gov/books/NBK19961/

50 https://www.pewresearch.org/social-trends/2009/07/29/nap-time/

51 https://www.mayoclinic.org/healthy-lifestyle/adult-health/in-depth/napping/art-20048319

52 http://www.eyewitnesstohistory.com/washington.htm

53 J Am Geriatr Soc . 2006 Jul;54(7):1142-3.

54 My Mother, Your Mother: Embracing "Slow Medicine," the Compassionate Approach to Caring for Your Aging Loved Ones Dennis Mccullough

55 https://www.nature.com/articles/s41598-020-75888-8

56 Tornstam, L., 1997 Gerotranscendence: The Contemplative Dimension of Aging The Journal of Aging Studies, vol. 11 2:143-154

57 https://mitpress.mit.edu/books/zen-and-brain

58 https://www.historyextra.com/period/victorian/prince-albert-the-death-that-rocked-the-monarchy/

59 https://www.ncbi.nlm.nih.gov/pmc/articles/PMC2784544/

60 (Evashwick, 1989)